The Slack Packer's Guide to Hiking the Appalachian Trail

The Slack Packer's
Guide to Hiking the
Appalachian
Trail

Lelia Vann
& Greg Reck

MARINER
PUBLISHING
BUENA VISTA, VA

1 3 5 7 9 10 8 6 4 2

Library of Congress Control Number: 2017903361
The Slack Packer's Guide to Hiking the Appalachian Trail
By Lelia Vann and Greg Reck

p. cm.
1. Sports & Recreation: Hiking
2. Travel: Special Interest—Hikes & Walks
3. Travel: Food, Lodging & Transportation—General

I. Vann, Lelia, 1958– II. Reck, Greg, 1946– III. Title.
ISBN 13: 978-0-9975226-3-1 (softcover : alk. paper)
ISBN 13: 978-0-9975226-7-9 (ebook)

Cover and Book Design by Karen Bowen

Mariner Media, Inc.
131 West 21st Street
Buena Vista, VA 24416
Tel: 540-264-0021
www.marinermedia.com

Printed in the United States of America

This book is printed on acid-free paper meeting the requirements of the American Standard for Permanence of Paper for Printed Library Materials.

Dedication

We dedicate this book to Adam DeWolfe aka Wolfman who saved us from hypothermia in 2016 on top of Franconia Ridge during an ice storm. Without his help, we would not be here today. Many thanks also go out to the New Hampshire Fish and Game Specialized Search and Rescue Team, Androscoggin Valley Search and Rescue, and Pemigewasset Valley Search and Rescue Team. They brought the equipment and personnel needed to get us below the tree line and back to safety.

Contents

ACKNOWLEDGMENTS   IX

INTRODUCTION   I

HOW WE PLANNED BEFORE WE LEFT   3

SAFETY   15

WHAT WE TOOK   21

COST   29

WHAT WE DID AND HOW WE PLANNED
ONCE ON THE TRAIL   31

SPECIAL SECTIONS   123

TRAIL NAMES GLOSSARY   133

APPENDIX I: DRAFT AT PLAN 2015   137

APPENDIX II: MAIL DROP LIST   171

Acknowledgments

The outdoors has always played a significant part in my life. As a child growing up in Alabama, my brother and I spent a lot of time exploring the woods behind our house. As I finished undergraduate school, I found myself taking up jogging and later cross-country jogging just for the fun of being outdoors. I remember thinking about how neat it would be to jog the entire Appalachian Trail one day, but after knee surgery in my fifties, I knew that would never happen. However, I feel fortunate to have thru-hiked the Appalachian Trail with my best friend and husband, Greg Reck aka Rocketman, and my brother, R. E. aka Ranger. I would not have completed the trail without either one of you.

I also want to acknowledge many others that helped us complete our thru-hike and encouraged us to write this book.

First, is our trail boss Alan Smith, who was always there to send us our mail drops, deal with issues at home, and just kept us informed and connected back home in Norfolk, Virginia. Ranger shuttled us from Springer Mountain, Georgia, to Fontana Dam in North Carolina. Gay Vann (Ranger's wife) welcomed us into their Georgia home, found us lodging in Georgia, supported us in Georgia, Tennessee, North Carolina, and Virginia, and allowed Ranger to hike with us in Virginia, New Hampshire, and Maine.

Marie at the Standing Bear provided shuttle service in the Max Patch area.

Daniel at The Bluff Mountain Outfitter in Hot Springs provided us with several early morning shuttle rides in the Hot Springs area. Special thanks to Biscuit, the owner of the Smokey Mountain Diner in Hot Springs, for allowing us to eat breakfast early so we could hit the trail early.

Mike and Peggy at Cantarroso Farm in Erwin, Tennessee, shared their beautiful home with us, shuttled us to and from the trail, and took us to dinner each night. In addition, Tom (10-K) and Marie Bradford were willing to shuttle us to and from the trailheads in the Erwin, Tennessee, area at a very reasonable price and early in the mornings.

Mary, Terry (in memory), Dave, and Shannon at the Mountain Harbour B&B and Hostel in Roan Mountain, Tennessee, were wonderful. Everyone pitched in to make us comfortable and Mary's gourmet breakfast was famous on the trail.

Mary Lee, Bob, and Stephanie at the Black Bear Resort in Hampton Cove, Virginia, accommodated our needs with a cozy cabin, early shuttles, food, and beer.

Vicky at the Iron Mountain Inn B&B in Butler, Tennessee, shuttled us to and from the trail, took us to dinner at a local Asian restaurant, and served us a fabulous breakfast at her quiet and romantic mountain home overlooking Watauga Lake.

Miss Ginny at the Lazy Fox Inn B&B in Damascus, Virginia, shared her lovely four-bedroom antique home and provided us with the best country-style breakfast you can find along the trail. Jeff and Dave (in memory), owner of the Mount Roger's Outfitter in Damascus provided us with reasonably priced shuttles with early start times, plus they have one of the best outfitters along the trail.

Grasshopper and Runaway (2014 AT thru-hikers) met us in Damascus and took us to dinner in Abingdon, Virginia.

Skip and Linda shuttled us to and from the trailheads in Atkins, Virginia. Bubba provided shuttles in both the Atkins and Bland area for a reasonable price. He was reliable and provided early shuttles.

Neville and Michael at Woods Hole provided us with breakfast, dinner, a nice bedroom, and shuttled our packs into Narrows for a modest fee.

Allen, the owner of MacArthur Inn in Narrows, Virginia, picked us up at the trailhead and took us to his hotel for the evening. Don Raines provided us with reasonably priced on time and anytime service in the Narrows and Pearisburg, Virginia, area.

Homer Witcher shuttled us from Sinking Creek to the James River Bridge. He was reasonably priced and would pick you up early.

Mary Stuart and Russ at 502 South Main B&B in Lexington, Virginia, provided a gourmet breakfast, one of the finest bath and bedrooms, and shuttle service while staying with them.

Mister Gismo provided us with shuttle service in the Waynesboro, Virginia, area. This included the southern end of the Shenandoah National Park. Bill and Nickie at the Tree Streets Inn in Waynesboro, Virginia, shared their nice, colonial-revival B&B and provided a nice breakfast before shuttling us to the Rockfish Gap trailhead.

Mike Evans shuttled us in the Front Royal area. His prices are reasonable and he knows the area well.

Karen Townsend at the Town's Inn in downtown Harpers Ferry, West Virginia, offers traditional rooms in her 1840 residence with a nice restaurant and outside patio area.

Dave and Margaret at the Burgundy Lane B&B in Waynesboro, Pennsylvania, served us a gourmet breakfast at our choice of time, shuttled us to and from the trailhead as part of the cost of our lodging, and had really nice and unique bedrooms and bathrooms.

Angel Mary reliably shuttled us in the Duncannon, Pennsylvania, area.

Joyce and Lance Carlin shuttled us in the Pine Grove, Pennsylvania, area—extremely reliable. Kenny at the Blue Mountain B&B in Andreas, Pennsylvania, provided us with a nice room and fine food and drinks.

Kathy and Sherri at the Filbert B&B in Danielsville, Pennsylvania, provided us with everything—nice elegant room, gourmet breakfast, loaner clothes, shuttles to dinner/store/trailhead.

Mary at the Deer Head Inn in Delaware Water Gap, Pennsylvania, provided us nice lodging and a fine dining restaurant on Thursday through Sunday Brunch with the best jazz along the East Coast.

Kenny shuttled us at anytime in Delaware Water Gap area.

Ron at the High Point Country Inn in Wantage, New Jersey, managed the inn and shuttled us to and from the trailhead.

Matt at Anton's on the Lake in Greenwood Lake, New York, owned and managed the lakefront room and shuttled us to and from the trailhead as part of our lodging.

Martin "the Edge" Hunley shuttled us from the Hudson River to Wingdale, New York. He and his wife, Donna, are the only Appalachian Trail shuttlers that we could find in this area. They are extremely nice, but they both have full-time jobs. He made it work for us by shuttling us before and after his working hours.

Cooper at the Cooper Creek B&B in Kent, Connecticut, shuttled us to and from the trailhead as part of our lodging. He made us breakfast and took us into town for supplies, laundry, and dinner.

Hudson and Big Lu at the Bearded Woods Bunk and Dine near Sharon, Connecticut, shuttled us to and from the trailhead, served gourmet-style dinners and breakfast, and provided nice clean lodging.

Jess Treat in Sheffield, Massachusetts, rented us a room in her home, prepared a hot breakfast each morning, and provided shuttle service to the trailhead and dinner in town.

David Ackerson shuttled our packs from Williamstown, Massachusetts, to our hotel in Bennington, Vermont.

John Perkins shuttled us from Bennington to Danby, Vermont.

Jeff and Regina Tausig host hikers at Green Mountain House in Manchester Center, Vermont, have a private room for couples. You have full kitchen privileges, and they will shuttle you into town for dinner and supplies.

Cathy at Silas Griffith B&B in Danby, Vermont, provided breakfast and shuttled us to and from the trailhead. She also drove us into town for dinner.

Plans Too Much and his wife shuttled us from VT 103 to Norwich, Vermont. He knew the trailheads well and was responsive to our requests.

Murray and Patty McGrath at The Inn at Long Trail in Killington, Vermont, have clean country-style rooms in a lodge. They served us breakfast, lunch, and dinner. The breakfast is included in the lodging. They also have an authentic Irish Pub.

Patrick at the Dowd's Country Inn B&B in Lyme, New Hampshire, prepared our breakfast and shuttled us to and from the trailhead each day. The rooms were very nice and clean.

Legion at Hike's Welcome Hostel in Glencliff, New Hampshire, held our full packs while we hiked. Josie Barnett (a NASA friend) and her friend Ivette Babylon shuttled us from the Hiker's Welcome Hostel in Glencliff, New Hampshire, to North Woodstock, New Hampshire, for dinner and lodging.

Kevin at the Gale River Motel in Franconia, New Hampshire, shuttled us to and from the trailhead. He also shuttled our packs to the Highland Center.

Marny at the White Mountain Lodge and Hostel in Gorham, New Hampshire, provided breakfast as a part of our lodging, shuttled us to and from the trailhead, and has a private room for couples.

Honey and Bear aka Margie and Earl at The Cabin in Andover, Maine, provided breakfast as a part of our lodging, provided dinner and shuttles for a fee, and had a private room for us. They made it possible for us to slack Mahoosuc Notch. Don, Margie's son, and Hopper, a friend, helped with the cooking, cleaning, and shuttling.

Shane and Stacy at the Farmhouse Inn in Rangeley, Maine, provided us a private room and shuttled us to and from the trail.

Susan in Stanton, Maine, shuttled us to and from the trail.

Eric at the Sterling Inn B&B in Caratunk, Maine, provided us with breakfast, a clean private room, and shuttled us to and from the trail.

Poet and Hippy Chick at Shaw's Hiker Hostel in Monson, Maine, provided us with a private room and shared bath. Dawn, Dick, and Gary near the Shaw's Hiker Hostel in Monson provided our shuttles from Moxie Pond, Maine, to half-way through the 100-mile Wilderness.

A special thank you goes to Joe Valesko, founder of Zpacks, for expediting our lightweight gear before and during our thru-hike.

Thanks to AWOL, author of *The AT Guide Northbound*, for such a great guidebook and being responsive when we had questions about the book.

We would like to thank the Appalachian Trail Conservancy for all they do to protect the trail from threatening projects like the Mountain Valley pipeline project, to keep the trail maintained, and to keep hikers informed about any hazards or safety issues so we can enjoy the outdoors. In addition, we would like to thank the Appalachian Mountain Club for their huts and lodges throughout the Whites and all they do to protect and maintain the trails of the White Mountains so we all can enjoy them.

Special thanks to Spartacus and Focus for joining us in Connecticut—plus Spartacus' wife, Janelle, and his friends, Penny and Rick, for sharing their lovely home and providing us with healthy food to fuel our adventure.

Warm thanks to Andy Wolfe, Karen Bowen, and Judy Rogers of Mariner Media for suggestions, careful attention to our text, patience, and your time.

Thanks to Jessica Treat, David Miller, Ray King, and Jim Smoot for reviewing our book and providing your thoughtful comments during your already busy schedules.

Introduction

When my husband, Greg (aka Rocketman), my brother, R.E. (aka Ranger), and I (aka Princess) decided to "thru-hike" the Appalachian Trail (AT) in 2014, I retired at the end of September 2013 to get ready. I spent five months dehydrating food and prepared twenty-one food drops for us between Georgia to Maine. Needless to say, within the first couple of months of our 2014 "thru-hike," we were sick of the food that I had prepared and started eating as many of our meals off the trail as possible. As a matter of fact, once I learned of "slack packing," I pushed to do that as much as possible, which was the best of everything in my mind—hiking but staying clean, eating regular food, and sleeping in beds.

Slack packing is to hike without a full pack and typically means you pay someone to shuttle you to and from the trailhead each day and stay in towns with B&Bs, hotels, and/or hostels. You take a daypack with enough food for the day, a minimal set of items for weather, and your safety. You can even afford to carry your water, so you don't need to worry about finding and filtering water along the way. Many thru-hikers will engage in slack packing as a treat, especially if it's offered as part of their stay at a lodge/hostel.

My brother decided to come off the trail in Harper's Ferry, which is referred to by many as the psychological "halfway" point. He was homesick and preferred to sleep in the woods instead of B&Bs, hotels, or hostels. So, my husband and I decided to finish the remainder of the trail by slack packing the rest of the way where possible. We were approached by others along the way who said they would consider thru-hiking if they could do it our way. They suggested that we write a book to share how to thru-hike the trail without carrying a full pack and without having to sleep in the woods.

After summiting Katahdin on August 19, 2014, my husband started pulling our story together as he had taken over 3,000 photos. In January 2015, we watched his slideshow. We had so many fond memories of the trail, people, towns, and experiences that we both wanted to go back. So, we decided to "thru-hike" the AT again in 2015. We set our goal to "slack pack" as much of the trail as possible, so we could write this book and keep track of the cost of doing it this way.

This book is a guide on how we approached our goal and presents our considerations with respect to shuttles, places to stay, mail drops, equipment, and hiking distances each day.

How We Planned Before We Left

"Must Have" Publications

Because we had already thru-hiked and slack packed almost half of those miles in 2014, we thought we had a good idea of how we should plan for slack packing the entire distance. First, I ordered the *AT Guide 2015 Northbound** (referred to as the *AT Guide* or AWOL's book), the complete set of AT maps, Guthook (electronic app), and a DeLorme *Gazetteer Atlas* for each state, so I could create a draft plan for our entire hike—starting in Georgia and ending in Maine.

In 2014, we ordered both AWOL's AT Guide *and the ATC's* AT Companion. *We liked the format of the* AT Guide *by AWOL much better, although both had most of the same information. You will need to decide which one you prefer but either the guide or companion is a MUST have.*

The *AT Guide* can be ordered online from www. theatguide.com. The *AT Guide Northbound* starts in Georgia and ends in Maine. (There is a southbound version that starts in Maine and ends in Georgia for those that plan to hike southbound.) Each year, <u>AWOL</u> sells an updated version because there are always changes in the trail route, lodging, etc. We bought a guide in 2014 and then another one in 2015. We also purchased the electronic version, which has hyperlinks to websites and telephone numbers. This type of guide is a "must have" if you plan to hike or slack pack the trail. It identifies

You can purchase a copy of the *AT Guide* at www.theatguide.com

AWOL's guidebook that we used.

major mile markers along the way with the elevation and includes all the road crossings, so you can decide on pick up/drop off points to/from the trail.

The complete set of AT maps (thirty-five maps) can be ordered online from the ATC website (www.appalachiantrail.org). Click on "shop," then "start shopping now." Click on "planning," then "Official A.T. Guide Sets." Select "Complete Set of Appalachian Trail Guide Books and Maps." The complete set of maps were $327.50 (at the time of this book's publication).

> Order AT maps at atctrailstore.org/
> planning/official-a-t-guide-sets/
> complete-set-of-appalachian-trail-
> guide-books-and-maps/

The maps were helpful in getting an aerial (map) view of where you were in a particular region, so you could see where the towns and roads were located. You could also see other trails, water sources, etc. I thought these would be most helpful if we ever got in trouble and needed to come off the trail, i.e. we would know where the nearest access points were and we could better communicate where we were. I divided these up and sent them in mail drops along the way, so I would not have to carry them all. I also divided AWOL's *AT Guide* book into sections and sent them along with the corresponding maps instead of carrying the entire book. (You can order AWOL's *AT Guide* book unbound, which makes it easier to separate.) The AT maps are not essential, but they did give us peace of mind about knowing where we were on the trail in case we were injured or needed help.

A complete set of AT maps that we ordered from the ATC. I numbered each map and put the corresponding AT mileage.

Smartphone App

The Guthook App is a smartphone application that has been developed for hiking trails such as the AT and others. (Search for "at hiker: guthook's guide" in the App Store.) There is an initial cost to purchase the application. In order to use the application on the AT, additional In-App purchases are necessary to buy a map for each section of the AT. The full length of the AT has been divided into ten section maps. I found Guthook to be extremely helpful during the hike, but it requires that a hiker carries a phone with the application and keeps the phone charged throughout the hike. Also, the hiker must load the appropriate map for the current section of the trail and change maps as required. A hiker should spend some time with the application to become familiar with the features.

Much of the information in the app is very similar to the information available in the AWOL's *AT Guide*, such as the trail elevation profile, shelter locations, water sources, trail and road crossings, etc. But, I found the app to be particularly helpful in two ways: (1) The app is extremely useful if you are concerned that you have "lost" the trail. On a few occasions, I suddenly realized that I had not seen an AT blaze for some time and I became concerned that I may have missed a turn in the trail and was wandering off-trail. The app uses GPS signals to identify the exact location of the hiker on the map view, and the hiker can immediately see on the map if she is on the trail or not. In addition, if the hiker is not on the trail, the app identifies how far the hiker is from the trail and the hiker can rotate their phone to identify which direction she should move to intersect the trial. (2) The app can also provide

Key

information on the trail distance from the hiker's location on the AT to any waypoint identified along the trail. For example, a hiker can determine the distance from her location to a particular water source, a shelter or a road crossing (either ahead or behind) in trail miles.

As noted, the hiker must have a phone with available power in order to use the app. But, phones are becoming very light, and an advantage of slack packing is that a phone can be recharged virtually every day while the hiker is sleeping off-trail. The app relies on GPS signals and does not require cell service, so it works virtually anywhere along the trail. And, the GPS feature can be toggled off when not needed saving additional power. I used an iPhone to take photos along the trail and turned it off when not using the camera or using the Guthook app. Also, I typically set my iPhone in "airplane mode" when not using it, and that ensured that I had power when I needed it.

A *Gazetteer Atlas* for each state can be ordered online at info.delorme.com

Atlases

The *Gazetteer Atlas* for each state (fourteen states) can be ordered online from the DeLorme website (info. delorme.com). These atlases were most helpful in giving me the big picture of where we were with respect to the major roads that were closest to the access trail points and the lodging towns we were staying in. Sometimes, I used these maps to help decide which town to stay in. For

example, we preferred staying in a place for
one night and we would use that location a

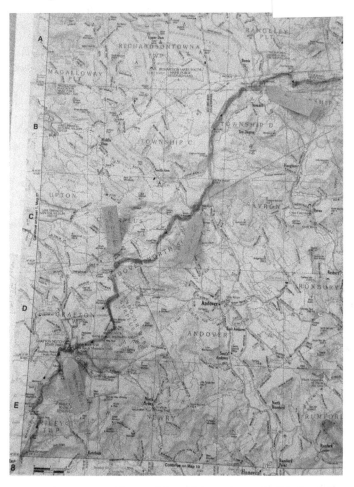

*A sample page out of one of the Atlases where I highlighted the
AT with a marker, identified major mile markers along the
trail with sticky arrows, and took a photo (with my iPhone),
so I could reference these maps while on the trail if needed.*

yes
?

we could leave our gear there while hiking. Our longest stay at one place was six nights. Many places were only two nights and the atlases helped in deciding which was better.

It turns out that there were only a few states where I really used these maps in planning, but I rationalized that they would be good for future road trips that we may take. In each atlas, I highlighted the AT with a marker, identified major mile markers along the trail with sticky arrows, and took a photo (with my iPhone) so I could reference these maps while on the trail if needed. I used the photos a couple of times to see major roads near towns because sometimes your plan doesn't work out and you need to replan. This really wasn't a major factor, but it was useful to have the data if needed. This was just a "nice to have" purchase. However, in 2016, we attempted our third AT thru-hike using our automobile. These atlases were "a must" if you plan to drive yourself to/from trailheads and lodging each day, or if you plan to have friends support you.

Emergency SOS Communicator

In 2015, we carried a DeLorme inReach SE satellite communicator every day. We learned about this system during our first AT hike (in 2014) and decided that we wanted an added measure of safety. Our primary interest in taking this device was to have a means of making an SOS call if we found ourselves in an emergency situation. This system employs a system of satellites that enables communication from virtually any point on the trail. This is different from cellphones that rely on cell tower service. Cell-tower communications may not be available at all points along the trail. The device that we purchased did not have voice communication capability, but an SOS could be initiated with a single button. And the device included a screen and keypad that could be used to send short text messages. The battery in the communicator lasted for several days and recharged quickly. We hoped never to need the SOS communicator, but later in 2016, we used it when we encountered extreme weather conditions in the White Mountains and had to be rescued. The only special condition on the communicator is that it must be carried on the outside of our daypack to enable visibility of the sky.

Draft Plan

Second, together with AWOL's *AT Guide* and our laptop, I generated our draft plan starting in Georgia and ending in Maine. (See Appendix I for our draft plan.) I started by looking for all the mile markers that have the parking icons and/or road crossings. I simply noted the distance between these points. I chose the mileage to hike based on the pick-up points available. For example, the closest parking lot to Springer Mountain (the AT southern terminus) is 1 mile away at Big Stamp Gap, USFS 42. So, I added an extra mile just to get to the starting point because we would need to go out and back. Many people start in Amicalola Falls State Park to hike the "approach trail" to Springer, but that adds an additional 8.8 miles to your start. We did not do this. Most people suggest that you start out with short distances, say 8 miles, and then work your way up as you build endurance and trail legs. By slack packing, you may be able to start with longer miles. I think it really depends on your physical conditioning and your goals.

If you wanted to start out by including the Approach Trail, your first day could be 9.8 miles to Big Stamp Gap, USFS 42. This would include 8.8 miles (Approach Trail) and 1.0 mile of the AT (Springer to Big Stamp Gap). As you can see, we decided to start at Big Stamp Gap, hike up to Springer, turn around and hike back past Big Stamp Gap onto Cooper Gap giving us a 13.3-mile day but only covering 12.3 miles of the AT. I started out labeling our first day as Day 1 and added the date we planned to start, and the total mileage for that day. I did this all the way to the end at Mount Katahdin, realizing that this was a draft plan and would most likely change many times during our hike. However, it was solid with respect to deciding our mail drops, what needed to be included for the most part and giving others a general idea of where we thought we would be in a given month. At the end of each day, I added information about our shuttler (or shuttle service), lodging, options, etc. I also included planned "zero" days or days that we were not hiking (rest days). Typically, on the hike, I updated this information to include what we actually did and paid for in shuttling and lodging.

Third, I numbered each AT map from 1 to 35 and then used AWOL's *AT Guide* to label each map with the AT mileage covered. For example, the first map was number 1 of 35 and covered 0–80 miles of the AT. Next, I inserted this information in our draft plan, so I would know which map covered each day's hike. This information was used to determine which maps and pages of AWOL's *AT Guide* needed to be included in each mail drop.

Fourth, after completing the draft plan with map coverage information and potential lodging and/or outfitter mail drop information, I created a mail drop list/plan. See Appendix II for our draft mail drop plan. I had seventeen planned drops. (Of course, I took the first drop with me.) I packaged each drop before we left home. I did not seal them just in case we needed to add something. I left this list with our Trail Boss. (A Trail Boss is someone that helps you along the way. In our case, our Trail Boss not only mailed each drop to us but also took care of looking through our mail. He was wonderful.) I will talk later about what we included in our mail drops, besides the maps and AWOL's *AT Guide* sections. We included the address and mail date. I did have to update this mail drop plan during the hike because we had to take some extra days off and other changes. We just made those changes and provided them to our Trail Boss with no issues. In addition, I did want to keep the maps, so I would mail them back home whenever we had covered that area. Many times, the places that we stayed would mail them back for a small fee if there were no post offices nearby.

Safety

A Few Words About Safety, Weather, Getting Lost, etc.

Hiker safety is of paramount importance on the trail. Several major factors that influence safety include weather, trail difficulty compared to hiker ability, losing the trail (or getting lost), and accidents or unpredictable events like snakebites, bee stings, illness, etc.

Weather is a major factor and arguably the most important factor for significant portions of the trail. Depending on the hiker's abilities, a slack packer will be on the trail for perhaps 6 to 12 hours. In our opinion, an early morning weather forecast for the same day is more accurate than a forecast for several days in the future. Even more important is that the hiker uses the best weather forecast source available. Also, hikers must be aware that weather conditions at higher elevations on the trail are likely to be more extreme than at lower elevations.

Weather resources are available that predict conditions at various points along the AT. A website at

.org provides location-specific forecasts
ional Weather Service. This site displays
forecast information for all the shelter
ng the AT. Also, weather conditions in the
White Mountains in New Hampshire are particularly
challenging and a website at Mount Washington
Observatory (www.mountwashington.org) provides a
"Higher Summits Forecast."

Be sure to check the weather. Get location specific forecasts from www.atweather.org

Key

Consult the weather forecasts daily and in particular, check the forecast first thing in the morning each day before the day's hike. An advantage of slack packing is that a hiker doesn't have to be on the trail every consecutive day. If the morning forecast indicates extreme cold or wind chill, extreme winds, thunderstorms, icing conditions, or other hazardous conditions, simply take a day off and wait until conditions are more acceptable for hiking. We have taken days off, for this reason, several times in 2015 and 2016.

The second factor noted above is trail difficulty compared to hiker ability. In general, hiking speed decreases as the trail difficulty increases. If a trail section is more difficult than anticipated, it will take the hiker longer than anticipated to complete the section. This can result in missing shuttle pickup or in a worst case scenario, night-hiking. However, the AT is one of the best-documented trails, so there should be no major surprises in trail difficulty. Resources such as AWOL's *AT Guide* provide elevation profiles and notations on special trail features. Hikers should also check Appalachian Trail Conservancy resources. For example, the ATC provides information on average hiking rates through various sections of the AT. Many hikers also use the blog sites available on the web such as Trail Journals or White Blaze. They identify specific hikers that are perhaps several days ahead and read their journal entries to gain information on specific trail conditions that they will soon encounter.

Also, it is wise to think ahead about a "Plan B" before starting. For example, what to do in case your progress is much slower than planned, or you don't reach the end point for the shuttle at the designated time. And each of us always carried a night-light and other gear that could be useful in unplanned situations. I also carried the AT map for the section of trail we were hiking because it shows other trails that we could potentially take if we got into trouble and needed to come off early.

A third factor to consider is losing the trail (e.g., missing a turn) or simply getting lost when you go off-trail to search for water or by-pass a trail obstacle. (Note that AWOL's *AT Guide* provides an elevation profile along the AT, but not a map.) We used the Guthook app on our iPhones (see the description in Smartphone Apps above) for these situations. The entire trail is well marked with white blazes (the Presidential Range in the White Mountains is a special exception). We did use the app occasionally when we drifted a short distance from the trail and also when we took a "blue blaze" spur off the main AT and were not sure which direction was northbound when we returned.

The last factor I suggested is unpredictable events. We both carried a number of safety-related items that might be helpful in unexpected situations. And we added several items after our rescue experience in 2016. As noted above, we always carried the local AT map in the event that we needed to get off the trail. If weather changes or precipitation were predicted, we also carried extra clothing items to address the variations. But we believe the most important safety item is the SOS satellite communicator that we always carried in the event of extreme life-threatening situations.

Two final guidelines that we try to follow is that we always start as early as daylight makes it possible to hike without a headlamp. And we always kept our "trail boss" up to date on where we were and what our plans were for the day. By starting at 6 or 7 a.m., we were able to finish our hike by early or mid-afternoon given our typical hiking speed. This gave us several hours margin of daylight in case we hiked slower than expected. And in summer months, thunderstorms often build up later in the afternoon. And if we do get into trouble, our trail boss is identified in our emergency contacts.

Lastly, there are natural hazards, such as bears and snakes, along the trail that are well documented in the Appalachian Trail Conservancy literature. One problem that Rocketman faced several times was tick-borne disease, Lyme disease in particular. We have identified several steps that we take to minimize the hazard from ticks: select light-colored clothing that makes ticks easier to see, wear long sleeves, tuck pant legs into boots and socks, and inspect yourself for ticks immediately after every hike (a good shower habit and enlist a friend's help if possible). Also, there are several tick repellent chemicals that can help. These are available in sprays and can also be used to pretreat clothing. But, read the instructions before using as these chemicals can cause health problems.

Even with precautions, ticks may still get through, so be vigilant to the symptoms of Lyme and related diseases. A large red mark or "bulls-eye" is one indicator of Lyme, but it does not always appear. On our initial hike in 2014, we never saw a tick on Rocketman or a mark, but suddenly he felt extreme muscle aches and weakness. And on our 2015 hike, we never saw a tick on him, but the characteristic mark appeared. Consult the AT website for more information about these issues.

Currently, we consult with our physician before our hike and carry a prescription for treatment in the event that we are suspicious that we may have been exposed to or contracted Lyme disease. We also carry prescriptions for treatment of giardia and minor infections. Another advantage of slack packing is that off-trail sites for medical issues are often readily available in the overnight towns for non-emergency diagnosis and treatment.

What We Took

How We Decided What to Take When

Because we had already thru-hiked and slack packed almost half of the miles before, we thought we had a good idea of what we should take for slack packing as much of the entire distance as we could. For example, we knew we would have to tent at least once in Georgia because of U.S. Forest Road closures before April 1 and all but one point in the Smoky Mountains (Newfound Gap). We really didn't know how many other nights we would need to tent, so we took as a minimum a sleeping bag, sleeping pad, and tent. We really did not know if there were other points in New Hampshire and Maine that we would have to tent, so we had these items in our backpacks the entire way just in case. Plus, we decided to start on March 1, so we knew we needed winter gear until mid/late April and then summer gear thereafter. For us, this meant different clothing and different sleeping bags. See below for our gear list.

Gear List
❄ = Winter gear   ☼ = Summer gear

Princess's List

    ULA cuben backpack

✗ ❄ Zpacks 20-degree bag w/cuben dry sack

✗ ☼ Zpacks 40-degree dual bag w/cuben dry sack

  ✗ Sea-to-Summit silk liner

  ✗ Sea-to-Summit sleep pad w/Sea-to-Summit dry sack

✗❄ Down booties

  ❄ Full length tights ✓

  ❄ Long-sleeve lightweight base layer top w/hood ✓

    Skort

    Lycra pantyhose (in summer I cut these above the knees and wore them as underwear under my skort)

    Lightweight gym shorts ✓

    Zpacks dry sack (w/flannel inside for use as a pillow) for clothes

    Long-sleeve Northface Thermoball hooded jacket w/Sea-to-Summit dry sack

  ✓Zpacks cuben poncho w/Sea-to-Summit dry sack

  ❄ Tall Outdoor Research gaiters

  ☼ Short Outdoor Research gaiters

    Darn Tough thin running socks—2 pairs

    Saloman trail running shoes

    Customed orthotics

    Biking gloves

  ☼ Outdoor Research arm warmers treated with InsectShield

  ❄ Wool arm warmers

✻ 360 earmuffs
    Bandana ✔
✿ Outdoor Research Rimmed hat ✓
✿ Sea-to-Summit head bug net treated with ✓
    InsectShield
    Smartwool mittens/gloves ✔
    Zpacks cuben mittens
    Black Diamond headlamp ✔
    Map(s) ✔
    AT Guide pages ✓
    Hiking poles ✓
    Granite Gear fanny pack ✔
    Rubbermaid small juice bottle w/carabiner
    iPhone w/charger ✔
*   Medical items w/Sea-to-Summit dry sack ✓
    Sea-to-Summit dry sack for snacks/food ✔
✻ Thermal Cup
    Sea-to-Summit titanium Spork w/carabiner
    Sea-to-Summit medium washcloth
    Sawyer mini-water filter and refill bag
    24 oz Smartwater sports bottle (at least 2)
    Spare eyeglasses in protective light weight case
** Personal items
    Sea-to-Summit daypack

*   Medical items: Epi-Pen, medical eye drops, leuko
    tape, blister Band-Aids, Band-Aids, corn discs,
    toe protectors, scissors, tweezers, Advil, Advil PM,
    allergy pills, peroxide wipes, pills for giardia, Lyme,
    urinary infection, pain
** Personal items: ID, medical card, credit card, small

amount of cash, wet wipes, Eucerin, cuticle cutters, toothbrush, toothpaste, floss, nail file, pumice stone, lip ointment stick on carabiner, insect repellent

Rocketman's List

Zpacks cuben backpack

Zpacks cuben tent w/titanium stakes

❋ Big Agnes 20-degree bag w/Sea-to-Summit dry sack

Sea-to-Summit silk liner

Sea-to-Summit sleep pad w/Sea-to-Summit dry sack

❋ Down booties

❋ Full length tights

❋ Long-sleeve lightweight wool base layer top

REI hiking pants w/removable legs

Zpacks dry sack (w/flannel inside for use as a pillow) for clothes

Long-sleeve Northface Thermoball hooded jacket w/ Sea-to-Summit dry sack

Zpacks cuben poncho w/sack

❋ Tall Outdoor Research gaiters

✿ Short Outdoor Research gaiters

Darn Tough thick hiking socks–2 pair

Saloman hiking boots

Sol insoles

✿ Outdoor Research Rimmed hat

✿ Sea-to-Summit head bug net treated with InsectShield

Smartwool mittens/gloves

Black Diamond headlamp

✿ Outdoor Research arm warmers treated with InsectShield

❄ Wool arm warmers
Buff w/fleece
Bandana
Gloves—2 different pairs
Zpacks cuben mittens
iPhone w/charger
Hiking poles
❄ Thermal Cup
Sea-to-Summit titanium Spork w/carabiner
DeLorme inReach SOS device w/charger
Nikon camera w/charger
❄ Jet Boil Stove w/fuel
Sea-to-Summit daypack

Type of Slack Pack We Used

We both started out using the Sea-to-Summit daypacks that compressed into a self-contained bag smaller than your fist. However, Rocketman switched to a runner's pack (Ultimate Direction Fastpack 20) with a hydration bag in Vermont, primarily for more comfort and fit. The straps on the Sea-to-Summit daypacks are thin and not padded, so they rubbed an abrasion on both his shoulders. I didn't have this problem, so I used the Sea-to-Summit daypack for the entire trek. I did, however, have to purchase a new one because the bottom of it wore thin in New England because I scooted over so many rocks.

The only problem I see using the runner's slack pack would be if you had to carry it in your regular backpack while hiking. For example, through the Smokies, we would have had to do this. However, by the time we reached Vermont, we knew we were most likely not going to have to carry/wear our regular pack anymore, i.e. (we arranged for) someone to take our regular packs from lodge to lodge for us for a fee. We really ended up using our backpacks as luggage to transport our personal gear from place to place. It's all about money. If you are willing to pay someone to transport your goods from one point to another, you could make any type of slack pack work!

What We Took Slack Packing

We both used hiking poles and wore biking gloves most of the time. We always took our thermoball jacket, poncho, water, and water filters just in case we got into trouble and had to stay out longer than planned. Fortunately, we never ran into this situation in 2015. (However, in 2016, we did. So I've added several items:

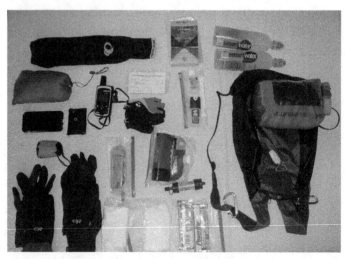

Rocketman's slackpack items.

SOL Emergency Bivvy, a ThermaCare Heat Wrap, and a headlamp.) I always took my Epipen, spare eyeglasses, and iPhone. Likewise, Rocketman always had his inReach, spare eyeglasses, and iPhone. See below for a list of what we carried slack packing. When slack packing you can afford the weight to carry your water, which saves time.

Princess: Sea-To-Summit Slack Pack
Spare eyeglasses in lightweight case
Emergency Thermal Blanket
EpiPen
Leuko tape
Map
Zpacks Poncho
Northface Thermoball Jacket with Hood in Dry
    Sack
Biking gloves
Arm warmers
24 oz Smartwater sports bottle filled with water or
    Gatorade (up to four depending on distance and
    weather)
Sawyer mini-water filter and refill bag
Hiking poles
* SOL Emergency Bivvy
* ThermaCare Heat Wrap (lower back and hip)
* Petzl Headlamp

Princess: Granite Gear Fanny Pack
2–3 energy bars depending on distance
iPhone
ID, medical card, credit card, small amount of cash

Few Advil
Wet wipes
AT Guide page(s)

Rocketman: Sea-To-Summit
(Later switched to Ultimate Direction Fastpack 20)
ID, medical card, credit card, small amount of cash
Spare eyeglasses in lightweight case
Zpacks Poncho
Northface Thermoball Jacket with Hood in Dry
    Sack
Biking gloves
Arm warmers
Sawyer mini-water filter and refill bag
1-liter bladder filled with H_2O
Snacks depending on distance
iPhone
inReach
Chargers for the electronic gear
Nikon Camera (waterproof, shockproof, and Wi-Fi-
    enabled)
Wet wipes
Hiking poles
* SOL Emergency Bivvy
* ThermaCare Heat Wrap (lower back and hip)
* Petzl Headlamp

Cost

The cost of shuttles and lodging was $20,000 ($6,000 and $14,000, respectively). Note that this cost does NOT include food or supplies along the way. Plus, the lodging can vary greatly. We preferred staying at B&B's, then hotels, then hostels. We also favored places that provided laundry service or at least were located near a laundromat. Although hostels are our least favorite places to stay, primarily because you typically sleep in a bunk room and share bathrooms with 8–12 other people. There were a few exceptions, like Woods Hole and Bear's Den in Virginia, Iron Master's in Pennsylvania, the Bearded Woods in Connecticut, the Green Mountain in Vermont, the White Mountain in New Hampshire, and The Cabin in Maine. In addition, many hostels have a private room that costs a little more but is well worth it for my husband and me to have the privacy.

The shuttle cost can vary depending on the shuttle driver. The typical charge was $1 per mile, but some charged up to $2 or more. Also, there was a difference between how they determined the distance charged. For instance, some charged the distance one-way, others charged two-way. Some charged the distance from their home to pick you up and take you to the trailhead, others would charge round trip. We did not call around and get the best price. We typically chose the shuttler that was recommended by others or the first one in AWOL's *AT Guide* book that we were able to reach and that was available to provide our shuttle request. We liked to hit the trail early and finish early, so we had time at the end of the day for cleaning up, doing laundry, running errands, and having dinner. Although there are shuttle drivers that are early risers, there are many that are not. I would call other drivers if the time for pickup was after 8 a.m. However, in some towns, there would only be one shuttle driver listed in AWOL's book. The Appalachian Trail Conservancy (ATC) also provides a list of shuttle drivers in each state. This list can be found on their website (www.appalachiantrail.org). Under "Explore the Trail" select "Transportation Options." On that page, scroll down to the section "Avoid Hitchhiking, Setup a Shuttle" and click on "AT Shuttles." The list starts on page 2 but there are good tips on page 1 that you should read as well.

Find a list of shuttles at
www.appalachiantrail.org/home/explore-
the-trail/transportation-options

What We Did and How We Planned Once On the Trail

From Springer (mm 0.0) to
Fontana Dam Visitor Center (mm 166.3)
166.3 miles

We were lucky in the first part of our hike because my brother, Ranger, offered to shuttle us from Springer to the Fontana Dam, which is the southern boundary to the Great Smoky Mountains—the first 166.3 miles. We parked our car at his house in Blue Ridge, Georgia, and he shuttled us from point to point. We stayed at his house for the first three nights, but as we got farther from his home, we stayed in lodging that was closer to the trailheads to minimize transport time.

During this 166.3-mile portion of the hike, we had to tent one night because the forest road that we had planned to use was closed to the public. The Georgia Forest Service roads typically open on April 1 but we started on March 1. (You can call the Georgia Forest Service at 770-297-3000 Monday–Friday to inquire about forest road status.) This was the section between Dicks Creek Gap and Wallace Gap—a 37.1-mile section. We tented at the Standing Indian Shelter, which made this a 16.7-mile hike from Dick Creek Gap, US 76, Hiawassee, Georgia, to the shelter and then a 20.4-mile hike the next day from the shelter to Wallace Gap, W. Old Murphy Road, Franklin, North Carolina. Then we stayed at a very nice cabin in

Fontana Village lobby—we stayed here in 2014. Nice accommodations just before you enter the Smokies.

Franklin for three nights, being shuttled to and from the trailhead by my brother. Our next move was to an inn in Bryson City, North Carolina, for three nights. Again, to position us closer to the trailhead and to minimize transport time to and from the trailhead each day.

During this period, I planned our next two sections: Gatlinburg in the Smokies and Standing Bear Farm in Hartford, Tennessee. I called the Grand Prix Motel in Gatlinburg to make reservations for two nights because I pretty much knew we could make it. I also let them know that we would want a shuttle back to the trailhead at Newfound Gap and which day. At this point, we also called Standing Bear to make reservations for two nights in their cabin or suites (not the bunkroom) and shuttles. I knew we wanted two shuttles and gave them those details to get their commitment. In addition, I called the Creekside Court in Hot Springs to make reservations for three nights. I knew we wanted to take another zero day and enjoy the Hot Springs. We also wanted two shuttles to Allen Gap during this time, so I called the outfitter and gave them our tentative plans. I would solidify once we made it to Hot Springs. At this point, if anything changes from your plan you should call and let folks know.

Fontana Dam Visitor Center (mm 166.3) to Hot Springs (mm 275.0)
108.7 miles

After Fontana Dam (mm 166.3), we entered the Great Smoky Mountains National Park. You will need a permit and need to pay a backcountry fee while hiking through this 69.4-mile section. There is an online system that allows you to pay and print a permit up to thirty days in advance (smokiespermits.nps.gov/index. cfm?BCPermitTypeID=1). A great place to register and print your permit is at the Nantahala Outdoor Center (NOC) outfitter at mile marker (mm 137.3), US 19 and 74 before you reach the Smokies. While hiking the Smokies, you will have to stay in their shelters. It's my understanding that there are four slots for thru-hikers in each shelter. This is important because the other slots are sold and reserved online, and if it's full, and there are four thru-hikers already in the shelter, you can be bumped out. You have to carry a tent just in case the shelters are full unless you reserve a spot in the shelter ahead of time. Plus, the rules state that you can only tent if the shelter is full.

The times that we hiked the Smokies coincided with college spring break, so the shelters were often full of students on spring break. Plan accordingly. The only road that you will cross in the Smokies is Newfound Gap, US 441, at mm 207.3. (There is a spur road from US 441 that goes up to the Clingmans Dome parking lot, and at mm 199.1, there is a side trail 0.5E to the parking lot but it is not open until April 1. However, this trail is only 8.2 miles from Newfound Gap, so if you start from Fontana Dam, you still need to tent unless you can hike 40 miles in one day with lots of ups and downs on rocky terrain.)

We entered the Smokies with our full packs knowing that we would tent two nights before coming off at Newfound Gap to stay in Gatlinburg, Tennessee. Our first section to Newfound Gap was 41 miles because we started at the Fontana Dam Visitor Center, which was a 1-mile hike to the Smokies southern boundary. The first day, we hiked 13.5 miles and stayed at the Russell Field Shelter. The second day, we hiked 16.7 miles and stayed at the Double Spring Gap Shelter. The third day, we hiked 10.8 miles to Newfound Gap where my brother's wife was parked to give us a ride into Gatlinburg. We stayed at the Grand Prix Motel, mainly because it was in Gatlinburg and easy to walk to places to eat. Plus they had a coin washer and dryer machine, which most of the hotels didn't have or advertise. The previous year we stayed at the Days Inn and had to take Gatlinburg's transit system to a laundromat. The total trip time was around three hours, which was not worth our time. Although the Grand Prix needed a face-lift, it was tolerable and the people were nice. They also provided a shuttle back to Newfound Gap for $30. We took two days off just to rest up.

The second section of the Smokies was 34 miles, so we decided we would spend another night in the woods and break this up into two days. (If you do the math, this section of the Smokies is only 29.4 miles, not 34, but we knew we wanted to stay at the Standing Bear Farm, so we hiked the additional 5.6 miles.) The first day, we hiked 15.6 miles and stayed at the Tri-Corner Knob Shelter. The next day, we hiked 18.4 miles to mm 241.3 at Green Corner Road and stayed in their "suite" at the Standing Bear Farm.

In 2014, we stayed in the cabin, which was nicer. In 2015, they built a small room (called a suite) overlooking a small creek on their property and we stayed in it. It was not completely finished. Although we prefer staying in the cabin, it has three beds so they would prefer renting it to a family or small group instead of just one couple. According to the *AT Guide* book, there was another place to stay but since we stayed here previously, we thought it was okay and liked the owners. Plus, they do shuttles early in the morning. However, one drawback is laundry. They only have a scrub board, but they do have a dryer that you can use. They also have a small room with a kitchen and a fairly well-stocked resupply, so you can cook yourself meals.

We stayed two nights at the Standing Bear. The next day (Friday), we were shuttled to Lemon Gap (mm 260.0) and hiked back to the Standing Bear, which was 18.7 miles. (Note that we walked South Bound (SOBO)

Creekside Court hotel in Hot Springs, North Carolina. Located in the heart of downtown Hot Springs. Near everything.

back to the Standing Bear. This makes logistics so much easier for you and the driver because they can just drop you off and you hike back. Otherwise, you would need to estimate how long it would take you to reach Lemon Gap and wait for a pickup.) The next day (Saturday), we were shuttled back to Lemon Gap, and we hiked 15 miles with our packs into Hot Springs (mm 275.0). Note, we could have paid Standing Bear to take our packs into Hot Springs, but we chose to hike with them, thinking we needed to carry our backpacks occasionally, so we could do it. We later got over this thinking.

Once in Hot Springs, we checked into the Creekside Court. We stayed here last year (2014) and thought it was located in a perfect spot—a laundromat to the left, the Bluff Mountain Outfitter (our shuttler) across the street, and the Spring Creek Tavern in front. After

Ranger, Rocketman, and Princess having breakfast at the Smokey Mountain Diner in Hot Springs, North Carolina.

doing our laundry, we had lunch at the tavern, and then we walked across the street to arrange for our shuttle the next morning to Allen Gap (mm 289.2) NC 208, TN 70. This little town has everything within walking distance. The next morning (Sunday), we walked to the Smoky Mountain Diner for breakfast (they actually open earlier than they advertise) and then back to the outfitter to catch our shuttle ride to Allen Gap. We hiked 14.2 miles back to Hot Springs. After doing our laundry and getting lunch, we decided to hit the hot springs at the Hot Spring Resort, Campground & Spa. My brother and his wife decided to surprise us and stayed with us on our day off. The next morning, he dropped us off at the trailhead at Allen Gap and took our backpacks to our next destination—the Cantarroso Farm in Erwin, Tennessee.

Once we reached Hot Springs, I called the Cantarroso Farm in Erwin, Tennessee, to make reservations for four nights and to talk about the shuttles we wanted. They had a private room that we opted for. I also called ahead to the Mountain Harbour B&B in Roan Mountain, Tennessee, to make reservations for three nights and to talk about the shuttles we wanted. They also had a private room that we stayed in the previous year that was available.

Hot Springs (mm 275.0) to
Roan Mountain (mm 393.9)
118.9 miles

On Monday, from Allen Gap (mm 289.2), we hiked 20.8 miles to Devil Fork Gap, NC 212 (mm 310.0). Mike, the co-owner of Cantarroso Farm, picked us up and shuttled us back to his property. We stayed in the upstairs room in their beautiful A-frame house that overlooked the Nolichucky River. We had our own private room and bath. It was nice. Last year, we stayed at Uncle Johnny's Nolichucky Hostel. Although we were able to get a private space at the hostel, it was not as nice as the farm. We ended up staying five nights at the Cantarroso Farm, including one zero day because of the weather. The day after our first night at the farm (Tuesday), we started at Devil Fork Gap and hiked 21.8 miles to Spivey Gap, US 19 W (mm 331.8), where Mike picked us up again and took us back to the farm. The second day (Wednesday), Mike dropped us off at Spivey Gap, and we hiked 11.1 miles into Erwin, River Road (mm 342.9). We started walking to the farm, and Mike picked us up and gave us a ride back. The third day (Thursday), Mike took us to Iron Mountain Gap, TN 107 (mm 363.1), and we hiked 20.2 miles back to Erwin. We called Mike, and he picked us up and took us back to the farm.

The weather forecast called for snow on the fourth day. It did snow, so we decided to take a zero that day (Friday). We contacted Mary, the Mountain Harbour B&B owner, and alerted them that we would be a day late. They were good with it since many people decided to stay with them an extra day due to the snowy weather. Mike didn't feel comfortable driving us to the trailhead the next morning because of the snow, so we called 10-K (a shuttle driver listed in AWOLs book and someone we used in 2014) and his wife, Marie, said she would take us back to the trail. So, the fifth (and final) day (Saturday), Marie picked us up at the farm and dropped us off at Iron Mountain Gap. We hiked 15.9 miles with

Left to right: Mike (co-owner Cantarroso Farm), Princess, Peggy (co-owner Cantarroso Farm), Maverick, Rocketman, and Wye Knot enjoying dinner at Primo's Italian restaurant in Unicoi, Tennessee.

Princess and Ranger in one of the cabins at Uncle Johnny's in Erwin, Tennessee, in 2014.

Our first slack packing experience (in 2014). 10-K (shuttle driver) picks up our packs at Spivey Gap, US 19W, so we can slack pack into Erwin, Tennessee. From left to right: 10-K, Princess, Ranger, and Route Step.

Marie (shuttle driver) and Ranger at the dairy den for coffee and milkshakes on our way to the trailhead in Erwin, Tennessee.

our packs to Carvers Gap, TN 143 (mm 379.0) where we were picked up by David, the Mountain Harbour owner's son, and shuttled to the Mountain Harbour B&B and Hostel.

Just a note about the Cantarroso Farm. The owners, Mike and Peggy, are wonderful people that own a really nice piece of property. They will provide rides into town for resupplies and dinner. They had dinner with us each night and enjoyed talking with the hikers. Peggy wants to thru-hike the AT when she retires. Mike is retired and provides the shuttles to/from the trailhead. He does charge per person to the trailheads (except the one from Erwin to his property, which is free with a stay at his place). I found this type of charge (per person) to be

Mary, owner of Mountain Harbour Bed & Breakfast and Hostel, serves a gourmet breakfast.

different than most other shuttlers, who will charge a fixed fee for a drive to the trailhead, usually up to four people, so you can split the charge four ways.

Once we checked into the Mountain Harbour B&B, we got cleaned up, and they did our laundry for us as part of our stay. We stayed here last year and a few things had changed. They opened a resupply store, and they served lunch and dinner for a modest price. Last year, they would drop you into town for an hour and let you get dinner and resupply. Mary prepares a gourmet breakfast, and it's one of the best on the trail. She does a great presentation and offers a variety of choices. This breakfast is included in the price of the B&B. It's extra if you choose to stay in the hostel. (We stayed here again in 2016, and Mary had retired. Her son, David, had taken over the business and handed over her breakfast recipes.)

We knew we would stay for three nights at the Mountain Harbour B&B, so we called the Black Bear Resort to get reservations for two nights, worked out shuttle details, and alerted them that Mary would be dropping off our backpacks while we were hiking. I also called the Switchback Creek Campground to make reservations there for one night. I knew that we would be in Damascus after that, and we enjoy staying at the Lazy Fox B&B, so I called Ms. Ginny to book several nights with her before she filled up (her southern style breakfast is legendary on the trail).

The next morning (Sunday), Mary shuttled us to Walnut Mountain Road (mm 404.2), and we hiked 10.4 miles back to US 19E and walked another 0.3 miles back to the Mountain Harbour B&B. The next day (Monday), she shuttled us back to Carvers Gap, TN 143 (mm 379.0), and we hiked 14.8 miles to US 19E and walked the 0.3 miles back to the Mountain Harbour B&B. The third morning (Tuesday), Mary shuttled us back to Walnut Mountain Road, and we hiked 14.3 miles to Dennis Cove Road, USFS 50 (mm 418.5) and then another 0.4 miles to the Black Bear Resort in Hampton, Tennessee. Mary shuttled our backpacks to the Black Bear Resort, so we did not have to carry them.

Roan Mountain (mm 393.9) to Damascus, Virginia (mm 470.2)
76.3 miles

Once we arrived at the Black Bear Resort, we checked in, solidified our shuttle requests for the next two days, and recovered our packs. After getting our showers, I did the laundry. They have a small resupply store with frozen pizzas, sandwiches, and snacks. They have a pizza oven, a microwave, small refrigerator, and a coffee pot with coffee grounds, so we were set for a couple of days. They have very small one-room cabins with two bunk beds (no linens so you need to use your sleeping bag and/or liners and your own pillow made from your extra clothes in a dry sack), a small table, a chair, and a heater. They are very clean. They have a separate bathhouse for the men and the women. (We did stay here again in 2016 and rented a small cabin that had a private bath, small kitchen, sofa, and a small bedroom with bedding.)

Originally, we had planned for our next lodging to be at the Switchback Creek Campground and I had talked to the owner a couple of times letting him know that we planned to stay there and would need to be picked up and then dropped back at the trailhead the next morning. When we started talking about the details, he said he could not take us to the trailhead until 9 a.m. I tried my best to get him to take us earlier, but he wouldn't budge. I called the folks at Mount Roger's Outfitters, and they said they would pick us up at TN 91 and take us to Damascus, so we decided to do that instead. I called Ms. Ginny at the Lazy Fox to see if we could arrive a day early, and she was fully booked, so I called the Dancing Bear B&B and booked a room for one night. Then I called the Switchback Creek Campground back to let them know that we no longer planned to stay with them and no longer needed their shuttle services.

The next morning (Wednesday) at the Black Bear Resort, we were shuttled to Wilbur Dam Road (mm 431.5) and hiked 13.0 miles back to Dennis Cove Road and then the 0.4 miles to the Black Bear Resort. The second day (Thursday), we were shuttled back to Wilbur Dam Road and hiked 16.1 miles to TN 91 (mm 447.6) with our backpacks, where we were picked up by Dave from the Mount Rogers Outfitter in Damascus, Virginia. Dave took us to the Dancing Bear B&B in Damascus. After getting cleaned up, I took our clothes to Crazy Larry's for laundry service. (The laundromat in Damascus has been closed since 2014. There are two hostels that provide laundry service for a fee.)

The next morning (Friday), Bill from the Mount Rogers Outfitters shuttled us back to TN 91, and we hiked 22.6 miles into Damascus (mm 470.2). We had made arrangements with the owner of the Dancing Bear B&B to leave our backpacks in her B&B until we hiked back. We picked up our backpacks, walked down the street to the Lazy Fox B&B, and checked in with Ms. Ginny for four nights.

Damascus, Virginia (mm 470.2) to
Atkins, Virginia (mm 523.8)
53.6 miles

Ms. Ginny has four bedrooms that she rents—three upstairs and one downstairs. We like the Fireplace Room because it's convenient to the shared bathroom upstairs and has a shower and a bathtub. The downstairs bathroom only has a tub—the biggest claw foot tub I've ever seen and used. We stayed upstairs in the Fireplace Room.

Damascus is a hiker's town. The trail goes down the middle of town, and Mount Rogers Outfitters is one of the best on the trail. The people are extremely knowledgeable of the gear that they sell and they provide shuttle service to/from the trailhead for a fee.

We knew we were staying with Ms. Ginny for three nights, so I called ahead and made reservations at the Comfort Inn in Atkins, Virginia, for three nights. I really didn't know if we were going to stay there for three, four, or five nights. Since this was a hotel with many rooms, I felt I could hold off on making a commitment until I talked with the shuttle drivers to know what could work best. I called Skip in Atkins to let them know our plans for arrival into Atkins and our shuttle requirements.

On Saturday, we took a zero day at the Lazy Fox after hiking 22.6 miles the day before. The following morning (Sunday), Bill from the Mount Rogers Outfitters shuttled us to VA 600, Elk Garden (mm 493.1), and we hiked 22.9 miles back to Damascus. The

Entering Damascus, Virginia.

Ms. Ginny, owner of The Lazy Fox Inn Bed & Breakfast, and my brother, Ranger, at breakfast.

Bill, shuttle driver from Mt. Roger's Outfitter in Damascus, Virginia, drops hikers off at White Mountain in Virginia—2014. From left to right: Runaway, Ranger, Bill, Grasshopper, and Princess.

Grayson Highlands wild pony just outside of the Grayson Highlands State Park in Virginia.

third morning (Monday), Bill shuttled us back to Elk Garden, and we hiked 17.1 miles forward to Fox Creek, VA 603 (mm 510.2) where Bill picked us up and took us back to The Lazy Fox Inn. The last morning (Tuesday) at The Lazy Fox, Bill shuttled us back to Fox Creek, and we hiked 13.6 miles with our backpacks to VA 670, South Fork Holston River (mm 523.8). Skip's wife, Linda, was supposed to pick us up but she wasn't there. We had no cell service, so we waited an hour before I started walking to see if I could either get cell service or find a house that would let me use their LAN line. I walked over a mile and finally found a house with someone home. They allowed me to use their telephone. I called Linda, and she had thought her husband had picked us up. She was clearly sorry and dropped everything to pick us up. By the time I made it back to our pick up point, Linda was there to take us to the Comfort Inn in Atkins.

Atkins, Virginia (mm 523.8) to
Pearisburg, Virginia (mm 634.9)
111.1 miles

Last year (2014), we stayed one night at the Relax Inn, which is located on the west as the trail crosses US 11. It was nasty. I got sick, and we moved to the Comfort Inn, which is 3.7 miles west on US 11. The Comfort Inn is relatively new, so the rooms are still really nice and clean. It does not have laundry, but there is a laundromat about a mile east of the Comfort Inn across from the Dollar General, so you can resupply while you do laundry. However, the laundromat is closed on Sundays.

Once we got to the Comfort Inn on Wednesday, we got cleaned up, and I headed to the laundromat to wash our clothes and then picked up a few items at the Dollar General. There was a Subway in the filling station and a diner near the Comfort Inn, so we ate there for most of our meals.

Then I got to work on our next several days by making reservations at Woods Hole for one night and the MacArthur Inn in Narrows for three nights. The owner of MacArthur Inn, Allen, will pick you up at the trailhead in Pearisburg for a small fee. I also contacted Don Rains for shuttles during this portion. We used him last year, and he was fantastic. He also would pick you up at any time in the morning and picked us up promptly after our hike.

On Thursday morning Skip took us back to VA 670, South Fork Holston River (mm 523.8), and we hiked 18.9 miles to VA 683, US 11 (mm 542.7) and got a bite at The Barn before calling Skip/Linda for pickup back to the Comfort Inn.

The next day, Friday, we took a zero and rested. The day after that, Linda took us to VA 42, O'Lystery Pavilion (mm 554.9), and we hiked 12.2 miles back to VA 683, US 11 and ate again at The Barn before calling Skip/Linda for a pickup back to the Comfort Inn.

The next day, Sunday, Bubba (another shuttle driver that's in the next town) shuttled us to VA 623 (mm 572.6), and we hiked 17.7 miles back to VA 42, O'Lystery Pavilion, where Skip picked us up and took us back to the Comfort Inn.

The next day, Monday, Bubba shuttled us back to VA 623, and we hiked 18.4 miles to the north end of VA 612 (mm 591.0). Bubba kept our backpacks and later picked us up at VA 612 and shuttled us to Trent's Grocery. Trent's has a room that they will rent out. It has two twin beds, a TV, refrigerator, microwave, bathroom, and washer/dryer. It's not the cleanest, but it worked for us. We stayed for two nights. Trent's also has a deli, and they serve good food. They even prepared a breakfast sandwich for us the night before since we left early each morning to hike. Bubba was one of the best shuttle drivers on the entire trip—he will pick you up as early as you want, and he is reliable and thoughtful. Great person!

On Tuesday morning, Bubba drove us back to VA 612, and we hiked 17.6 miles to VA 606 (mm 608.6). Then we walked 0.5 miles west back to Trent's. We talked to Trent's owner about shuttling our backpacks forward to Woods Hole Hostel in Pearisburg, Virginia. He said he would for a fee, so the next day (Wednesday) we just walked the half

Bubba and Skip—shuttle drivers in the Atkins, Virginia area. From left to right: Princess, Bubba, Skip, and Ranger.

mile on VA 606 to the trail and hiked 15.2 miles to Sugar Run Gap, Sugar Run Road (mm 623.8). Our backpacks were there when we arrived.

We stayed at Woods Hole Home and Hostel last year (2014). They have a bunkhouse, and they have two rooms inside their house that they rent. One of the rooms in the house has three beds (two twins and a double) and the other room has a queen-size bed. We took the queen bedroom. Neville is a sweetheart and is the granddaughter of the original owner of the hostel. She and her husband, Michael, are massage therapists and for a fee will give you the works. Neville is a great cook. She provides breakfast and dinner for a fee. They have a small farm with livestock, chickens, gardens, etc. She would like to become self-sufficient, but they aren't there yet. We do get fresh eggs, garden grown vegetables, etc. when we eat there. You can also have your

Woods Hole main cabin in Pearisburg, Virginia, near Sugar Run Gap.

The MacArthur Inn in Narrows, Virginia.

laundry done for a modest fee. We only stayed there one night this year.

The next day, Thursday, we hiked 11.1 miles from Sugar Run Gap to Lane Street (mm 634.9) and called Allen at MacArthur Inn for a pickup. He was there within five minutes and drove us the 3.6 miles to the inn. Neville took our packs to the inn for a small fee while we were hiking, as she needed to go into town for another reason. We stayed at MacArthur Inn last year after hearing not too pleasant comments about the lodging in the town of Pearisburg. The MacArthur Inn is a historical building, so the rooms are somewhat dated, but they are clean. We like it because there is a small grocery, good restaurant, and a clean laundromat across the street. The inn serves breakfast but opens too late for us. They serve a special dinner on Mondays and Thursdays, which is quite good. (By special, I mean there is only one option for dinner like the surf and turf special with a side salad, baked potato, green beans, and vanilla ice cream for $14.95.) Get there early because they usually sell out.

Pearisburg, Virginia (mm 634.9) to
Across the James River Footbridge (mm 784.4)
149.5 miles

The next morning, Friday, Don Rains shuttled us to Stony Creek Valley, VA 635 (mm 654.7). We hiked 19.8 miles south back to Lane Street, where Allen picked us up and took us back to the inn. We used Don as our shuttle driver in this area last year. He will pick you up at any time and take you anywhere. His prices are reasonable, and he is prompt. He knows the area well and he knows where you get cell coverage. We asked him about moving forward and when it made sense to switch drivers and move on to the next town. He suggested Homer in Daleville as our shuttle driver and Craig Creek Road, VA 621, as our transition point to Homer.

I called Homer and told him that we were trying to slack as much of the AT as possible and that we wanted to write

Princess enjoying Trail Magic by Coffee Grounds at the VA 621, Craig Creek Road trailhead.

a book about it. He said he could slack us from Craig Creek Road, VA 621 (mm 686.7), all the way to the James River Bridge and US 501, VA 130 (mm 784.4). At that point, it would make sense to transition forward to another shuttle driver in the Buena Vista area.

The next morning, Saturday, Don shuttled us back to Stony Creek Valley, and we hiked 20.6 miles north to Sinking Creek, VA 42 (mm 675.3), where Don picked us up and took us back to the inn.

The next morning, Sunday, Don shuttled us back to Sinking Creek, and we hiked 11.4 miles north with our full packs to Craig Creek Road, VA 621 (mm 686.7). We arrived at Craig Creek Road a little earlier than we had communicated to Homer, so we had to wait just a few minutes on him. Homer drove us to the Howard Johnson (HOJO) in Daleville where we rented a car and drove home for a prescheduled dental appointment. So,

Princess with Don Raines, shuttle driver in Pearisburg, Virginia, area, whose motto is "Anytime, anywhere!"

we had two zero days (Monday/Tuesday). We stayed at this HOJO last year, and it was in the need of a face-lift. They only had one working washer and a dryer that was temperamental. The Super 8 across the street had a newly renovated sign on their marquee. We walked over there to check them out. The manager showed us a room, and we decided we would stay there when we returned from our trip home. We made reservations for five nights and used this as our home base in Daleville. This town has a Kroger, outfitter, restaurants, and an urgent care all within a mile radius. The Super 8 had a coin-operated washer and dryer that was available when I needed it. Homer was another shuttle driver that was available anytime and anywhere. He even offered us the use of his car while we were in town, but we declined

Princess with Homer, shuttle driver
in Daleville, Virginia, area.

since there were plenty of good restaurants within walking distance.

At this point, we knew how long it would take us to get to the Buena Vista area, so I called 502 South Main B&B in Lexington, Virginia, and made reservations for four nights. We stayed there last year, and it was fabulous. The owners are just nice people, and their home is immaculate. Lexington is 15 miles from Buena Vista, but there was not a lot available in Buena Vista. Lexington is a nice college town with plenty of nice restaurants to choose from. There is a local brew pub downtown as well. Everything is within walking distance. Homer also suggested we talk with Gary for shuttling us from the Buena Vista area. We knew about how long it would take us to get to Waynesboro, so I called the Tree Street B&B and made reservations for five nights. I

Princess on McAfee's Knob—one of the most photographed spots on the AT—in Catawba, Virginia.

also knew that once we reached Rock Fish Gap, there would be a list of shuttle drivers for that area who we could use.

Once we returned to Daleville from our trip home, we checked into the Super 8 on Tuesday.

On Wednesday morning, Homer picked us up at 6 a.m. and dropped us off at VA 785, Blacksburg Road (mm 703.7), and we hiked southbound 17.0 miles back to Craig Creek Road, VA 621 (mm 686.7). Homer picked us up and took us back to the Super 8. The next morning, Thursday, Homer picked us and drove us back to VA 785, and we hiked 24.1 miles to Daleville, US 220 (mm 727.8) where we were staying. The next morning, Homer drove us to Bearwallow Gap, VA 43 (mm 749.4), and we hiked southbound 21.6 miles back to Daleville, and we walked back to Super 8. On Saturday morning, Homer drove us to BRP 76.3 (mm 769.7),

502 South Main: A Bed & Breakfast in Lexington, Virginia.

and we walked southbound 20.3 miles to VA 43 where Homer picked us up and took us back to Super 8. The next morning (Sunday), Homer drove us to BRP 76.3, and we hiked northbound 14.9 miles to US 501, VA 130 (mm 784.6), where Homer's wife, Theresa, picked us up and took us and our backpacks onto 502 South Main B&B in Lexington.

James River Footbridge (mm 784.4) to Rockfish Gap (mm 861.7)
77.3 miles

At this point, we knew we wanted to stay at the Skyland Lodge in the Shenandoahs, so we called ahead and made reservations there for three nights. We enjoy staying at the lodge but they do not have laundry service, so you have to be okay with washing your clothes in the sink and hanging them

Rocketman and Princess on the James River Foot Bridge in Snowden, Virginia, the longest footbridge on the AT.

Mary Stuart, co-owner of 502 South Main Bed & Breakfast, refilling our water glasses at breakfast.

up to dry while staying here, or make other arrangements. We do enjoy the restaurant and bar. The food is good but you do pay more than you would in town. You need to call early for reservations. We prefer staying in the Pinnacle section of the lodge. The rooms have been upgraded and they are very close to the restaurant/bar.

On Monday morning, Gary's wife, Susan, picked us up from 502 South Main B&B and shuttled us to US 501, VA 130 (mm 784.6). We had planned to hike to US 60 (mm 806.4) but only made it to BRP 51.7 (mm 795.5) because Rocketman's leg was hurting and we realized it looked and felt like the beginning stages of cellulitis. He had it last year and had to come off the trail for a few days and take antibiotics. We called Mary Stewart, owner of the B&B, and she dropped everything to pick us up at the next road crossing, which was the Blue Ridge Parkway mile marker 51.7. We hiked 10.9 miles instead of our planned 21.8 miles. Mary Stewart took us straight to the emergency room (ER) where Rocketman was prescribed antibiotics and rest. We decided to take three zero days, so Rocketman could recover and then move on to Waynesboro, because the 502 South Main B&B was already fully booked for the weekend, and we had already made reservations at the Tree Streets Inn B&B in Waynesboro. Because we live in Virginia, we knew we could easily come back to Lexington and make up what we missed.

(We came back to 502 South Main in Lexington in early November 2015 to finish up the 36.3-mile portion from BRP 51.7 to VA 56, Ty River. We did the section in three days. Staying three nights in Lexington was nice, as the restaurants are top notch and we enjoyed going back. Plus, Mary Stewart and Russ are terrific hosts and their B&B is top of the line.)

On Friday, Gary picked us up after taking three full days off and took us to VA 56, Ty River suspension bridge (mm 831.8), where we hiked 15.5 miles north to Dripping Rock, BRP 9.6, (mm 847.3). Gary was there to pick us up and take us on to Waynesboro to the Tree Streets Inn.

We stayed at the Tree Streets Inn last year. It's a B&B located near downtown and close to Krogers, restaurants, and the laundromat. The owners are nice and will pick you up at Rockfish Gap trailhead only. Any other shuttles you need to arrange separately and there are many other drivers. There is a list of shuttle drivers posted on the trail at the roadside railing as you reach Rockfish Gap. They do not offer laundry, so you will need to take your clothes to the laundromat each day. It's not a bad walk and there is a nice little burger joint across the street, where you can grab a beer while you wait on your laundry.

We called Mister Gizmo (on the list) about shuttling us while we stayed in Waynesboro. He was only available for the next two days and suggested that we use Kathy (on the list) for the next several days. Kathy was only available for two days so I tried several others on the list. Debby was available for one day. Then I got lucky and my brother, Ranger, and his wife decided to join us for the remainder of the Shenandoah National Park.

The first morning in Waynesboro (Saturday), Mister Gizmo picked us up at the Tree Streets Inn and took us back to Dripping Rock, BRP 9.6, (mm 847.3). We hiked 14.4 miles to US 250 Rockfish Gap (mm 861.7) and then walked to the Welcome Center where we called Bill at Tree Streets to pick us up. We also bought some fresh popcorn to eat while we waited.

Rockfish Gap (mm 861.7)/Shenandoah National Park to VA 602 (mm 968.0)
106.3 miles

The next morning, Sunday, Mister Gizmo picked us up and took us to Skyline 90, spur trail from Riprap parking (mm 878.7), and we hiked 17.0 miles back to Rockfish Gap (mm 861.7) where we called Bill to pick us up and take us back to the Tree Streets Inn.

Rocketman's leg started swelling and hurting him again, so we decided that I would continue hiking until he got better. Then we would come back later for him to make this section up. This way I could shuttle him, as shuttling is expensive and more difficult to work having to drive up and down the Skyline drive at 30 to 35 mph with limited access points.

The next morning, Monday, Kathy picked me up and took me to Skyline 77.5, Ivy Creek Overlook (mm 893.9), and I hiked 15.2 miles back to Skyline 90, spur trail from Riprap parking (mm 878.7) where Kathy came to take me back to Tree Streets Inn.

The next morning, Tuesday, Debby took me to Skyline 65.5, Swift Run Gap (mm 907.1), and I hiked 13.2 miles back to Skyline 77.5, Ivy Creek Overlook (mm 893.9), where Debby came to take me back to the Tree Streets Inn.

The next morning, Wednesday, Kathy took me to Skyline 65.5, Swift Run Gap (mm 907.1), and I hiked 17.0 miles to Big Meadows Wayside (mm 924.1). She took Rocketman and our backpacks to the Skyland Lodge. She later came back to pick me up at Big Meadows and take me to the Skyland Lodge.

I knew from last year that the Skyland Lodge had no laundry services, so I had planned to hike from the lodge back to Big Meadows the next day, Thursday. Big Meadows has a laundromat and showers, so my plan was to carry clean clothes and shower and do my laundry at the end of my hike. My brother and his wife were scheduled to pick me up that afternoon, so I had plenty of time to hike 7.2 miles, get cleaned up, do my laundry, and walk a mile to the Big Meadow wayside where I could grab a bite and drink a beer. However, when I reached the Big Meadows campgrounds, I discovered that they were renovating their shower and laundry facilities, so I just walked on to the wayside and waited for my brother. We returned to Big Meadows later that year (October 2015) and the renovations were complete, so we were able to do our laundry.

While we were in the Shenandoahs, the Skyline drive tunnel collapsed and was closed making the shuttles north of Skyland Lodge more difficult because one had to drive around to pick up or drop on the other side of the tunnel. Essentially this added another hour to the already long shuttle. Again, we were lucky to have my brother and his car to assist.

The next morning, Friday, my brother and I hiked 18.3 miles from the Skyland Lodge (mm 932.0) to Elkwallow Wayside (mm 950.3) where Rocketman picked us up in my brother's car.

We called the Quality Inn in Front Royal to reserve one night there after leaving the Shenandoahs. I also called the Terrapin Station Hostel and made reservations for two nights. Mike, the owner, would not allow dogs, so we stayed in the Quality Inn one night since my brother has two dogs.

The next morning, Saturday, my brother and I hiked 17.7 miles from the Elkwallow Wayside (mm 950.3) to VA 602 (mm 968.0) with Rocketman shuttling us. We stayed one night at the Quality Inn. They have a coin operated washer and dryer and are located within walking distance of several restaurants.

The next day, Sunday, my brother shuttled Rocketman and me to VA 602 (mm 968.0) and took our backpacks to the Terrapin Station Hostel. Later, Mike picked us up at Tucker's Lane (mm 977.8) after hiking 9.8 miles. This was Rocketman's first day back after taking six zero days. (In October, we came back to Shenandoah for Rocketman to make up the section that he missed and we used our car for transportation to and from the trail.)

VA 602 (mm 968.0) to
Pine Grove Furnace State Park (mm 1102.0)
134.0 miles

We stayed at the Terrapin Station Hostel last year (2014). Mike, the hostel owner, thru-hiked the AT previously and understands hikers. He also knows the trail in his area really well and can get you to and from the trail with no problem. He will also take you into town for resupply and dinner. He has a washer and dryer that you can use. He will provide you one free shuttle with a two-night stay. Overall, a great person and host. This is a hostel, so you do not have privacy. You are in a bunkroom arrangement, and everyone shares one bathroom with a shower. Plus what cleaning is done is by the guests.

I called the Bears Den, made reservations ahead for one night, and asked for their private room. I also called the Town's Inn in Harper's Ferry for reservations for two nights. We asked Karen, the owner, about shuttling. She gave us the name of her driver and his contact information. I called Hal and talked with him about our shuttle requirements, and he assured me that he could accommodate us into Pennsylvania. We knew I had another doctor's appointment and needed to head home for a couple of days. I also reserved the Town's Inn for another two days once we returned from our trip home.

From left to right: Mike (shuttle driver and owner of the Terrapin Station Hostel in Front Royal, Virginia), Lady Moose, Ranger, and Princess.

The next day, Monday, Mike took us to VA 601, Blueridge Mountain Road (mm 989.6), and we hiked 11.8 miles back to Tucker's Lane (mm 977.8) where Mike picked us up and took us back to Terrapin Station. Rocketman was hurting, so Mike took him to their Urgent Care where the doctor put him on stronger antibiotics—Zithromax (Z-Pak).

Mike was a great host and took us to a restaurant both nights. The first night he just had a beer, and the next night he let us treat him to dinner. It was terrific.

The next morning, Tuesday, Mike took us back to VA 601, Blueridge Mountain Road (mm 989.6), and we hiked 13.3 miles to Bears Den (mm 1002.9). Mike took

Bears Den Hostel—a castle-like stone lodge owned by the Appalachian Trail Conservancy and operated by the Potomac Appalachian Trail Conservancy in Bluemont, Virginia.

our backpack to Bears Den while we hiked. We stayed at Bears Den last year and loved it. It's owned by the AT Conservancy and operated by the Potomac Appalachian Trail Club. They have a bunkroom and a private room—both are really clean. We enjoyed the private room with our own bathroom. They also have a washer and dryer that you can use, and they sell pizzas, ice cream, and other snacks. They provide the supplies for pancakes in the morning and coffee with the use of their kitchen. In addition, for $10, they will carry your backpacks into Harper's Ferry and leave them at the AT Conservancy, which is located uphill from the Town's Inn where we were staying.

Because Rocketman's leg was still trying to heal, we decided to break the next section to Harper's Ferry into

Rocketman, Princess, and Ranger at the Appalachian Trail Conservancy in Harpers Ferry, Virginia.

two sections. On Wednesday, we left Bears Den and hiked 14.2 miles to Keys Gap, WV 9 (mm 1017.1) where Hal picked us up and took us to the ATC HQ to pick up our backpacks and then to the Town's Inn in downtown Harper's Ferry.

On Thursday morning, Hal picked us up at the Town's Inn, dropped us at Keys Gap, and we hiked back to Harper's Ferry and to the Town's Inn. We stayed at the Town's Inn in downtown Harpers Ferry last year and enjoyed it. Karen is the owner, and she has three rooms. We like the one on the third floor because it's the largest and most private. However, its bathroom is on the second floor, but you do have a key and can keep it locked to keep others out. The inn has a restaurant and they are open from 6 a.m. to 10 p.m. The food is very good. They also serve beer and wine. The staff is excellent and very hard working. They provide laundry service for a modest fee. We enjoy being downtown and sitting on the front porch to eat at their two top. Since our 2015 stay, Karen has added a hostel next door to her B&B.

The next morning, Friday, Hal picked us up and took us to the rental car location, so we could drive home for our appointments. We took four zero days. This gave us plenty of time to make our doctor appointments, and Rocketman was able to get in to see his primary care physician. He needed the four days to let his leg continue to heal.

I called ahead to the Burgundy Lane B&B in Waynesboro, Pennsylvania, and reserved three nights. I also talked with the owner, David, about shuttling. He said he could accommodate our needs with our stay.

We returned to Harpers Ferry on Monday, and Hal picked us up at the rental car location and took us back to the Town's Inn. The next day, he shuttled us to Turners Gap, US Alt 40, (mm 1040.9), and we hiked 17.5 miles back to Harper's Ferry, High Street (mm 1023.4).

On Thursday morning, Hal picked our packs and us up and dropped us off at Turners Gap, US Alt 40, (mm 1040.9) and took our packs onto the Burgundy Lane B&B in Waynesboro, Pennsylvania. We hiked 13.4 miles to Wolfsville Road, MD 17 (mm 1054.3) where David picked us up and took us to his B&B.

We were pleasantly surprised with the Burgundy Lane B&B and the town of Waynesboro. The B&B was conveniently located with short walking distances to

Burgundy Lane Bed & Breakfast in Waynesboro, Pennsylvania.

restaurants and bars. The people were friendly. The B&B hosts (David and Margaret) were fabulous. They make sure their guests feel at home. They did our laundry. They served us breakfast at 5:30 a.m., so we could hit the trail by 6:30. They were just awesome. David shuttled us as part of the cost of the B&B, which was very generous. The rooms were extremely clean and comfortable. They provided a guest refrigerator and microwave in the upstairs hallway. It was all nice. Our room had access to a covered deck where we enjoyed sitting/resting after our hikes. (We stayed here again in 2016—the Castle Room, which had it's own refrigerator and microwave.)

I called ahead to the Ironmasters Mansion to make reservations for one night and to see if they could shuttle

The Castle Room inside the Burgundy Lane Bed & Breakfast in Waynesboro, Pennsylvania.

our bags to Allenberry on Saturday. I asked for the private room and was able to get it. Otherwise, they have two large bunkrooms—one for the males and the other for the females. The private room has a sofa that pulls out into a bed. The room is clean and has a private bathroom.

Pine Grove Furnace State Park (mm 1102.0) to Delaware Water Gap (mm 1277.8)
175.8 miles

On Wednesday, we jumped ahead to do 15.1 miles in dry weather, so David dropped us off at Mentzer Gap Road (mm 1067.1) and later picked us up at US 30 (mm 1082.2) and took us back to the B&B. The next morning, Thursday, we hiked 12.8 miles and made up the section we skipped from Wolfsville Road, MD 17 (mm 1054.3) to Mentzer Gap Road (mm 1067.1). David picked us up and carried us back to the B&B.

On Friday morning, David dropped us off at US 30 (mm 1082.2) and took our packs on to the Ironmasters Mansion at the Pine Grove Furnace State Park. We hiked 19.8 miles (mm 1102.0) to the Ironmasters Mansion and the Pine Grove General Store, which is located next door. The Pine Grove General Store is the home of the half-gallon ice cream challenge. We ordered our ice cream and stayed on the benches at the store until the Ironmasters Mansion opened for check-in.

The caretakers (Mike and his wife) at the Ironmasters Mansion were very nice and accommodating. We stayed there last year and enjoyed our stay, so we decided to stay again. The caretakers changed, and we liked them. We had already made arrangements with Mike to take our packs to Allenberry Resort the next morning while we hiked. The only drawback to staying at the Ironmasters is that you can't check in until 5 p.m., which means you sit around at the store or go to the museum until they open. The general store does have good food. The Ironmasters does provide a continental breakfast, and you can do your laundry there, but again, if they opened earlier it would be much more convenient for early risers.

The next morning, Saturday, we left our backpacks with Mike, and we headed out for our 19.3-mile hike into Boiling Springs (mm 1121.3). We had already called ahead and made reservations at the Allenberry Resort. We stayed there last year and liked the restaurant/bar. You have to walk another half mile off trail to the resort. The hotel is clean and they do have a washer and dryer in the basement that you can use. (We understand that the Allenberry Resort was for sale in 2016 and not being maintained. We stayed at a B&B in Boiling Springs in 2016, but it wasn't the best place either.)

Our next segment would be into Duncannon, and this is where the Pennsylvania rocks start. We had also planned to take a zero day in Harrisburg, Pennsylvania, and stay at the Riverfront Comfort Inn in downtown Harrisburg. We stayed there last year and enjoyed the town. We arranged with Angel Mary in Duncannon to pick up our packs at The Allenberry Resort in Boiling Springs, then pick us up in Duncannon at the Doyle, and then shuttle us on to Harrisburg.

On Sunday morning, we hiked out of the Allenberry Resort, PA 174 (mm 1121.3). We hiked 25.6 miles to Duncannon, Pennsylvania, (mm 1146.9) and stopped in at the Doyle for a beer and something to eat, while we waited for Angel Mary to take us to the Riverfront Comfort Inn in downtown Harrisburg. We stayed at the Doyle one night last year (2014), and I wouldn't recommend it to anyone. Everybody shares one bathroom that has only one shower, one sink, and one toilet. It's not pretty—it's nasty.

The next morning, Monday, we took a zero and enjoyed downtown Harrisburg.

On Tuesday morning, Angel Mary picked us up and took us to PA 325, Clarks Creek (mm 1164.6), and we hiked 17.7 miles SOBO back to Duncannon (mm 1146.9), where we got a drink and something to eat while waiting for Angel Mary to shuttle us back to Harrisburg.

On Wednesday morning, Angel Mary picked us up in Harrisburg and took us back to PA 325 (mm 1164.6). She kept our packs while we hiked 16 miles and then picked us up at PA 443, Lickdale (mm 1180.6) and took us to the Days Inn, Lickdale. We weren't that familiar with this area even though we stayed in Lickdale at the Comfort Inn last year. The Days Inn was a little closer to the places to eat, yet both had coin laundry. We decided we would move on to the Comfort Inn, Pine Grove, Pennsylvania, the next day.

We made arrangements for Joyce and Lance Carlin to shuttle us for the next few days. Our next stay would be at the Comfort Inn, then on to the Union House B&B in Port Clinton, Pennsylvania. I called ahead and made reservations for our stay. The Comfort Inn didn't have laundry, but there was a Pilot Travel Center within walking distance, so we did our laundry there while we ate at the diner next door. Last year, we stayed at the Hampton Inn, which was very nice. Not sure why we changed it up.

On Thursday, Joyce picked us up at the Days Inn and took us (and our backpacks) to the trailhead at PA 443 (mm 1180.6), and we hiked 12.8 miles to PA 501 (mm 1193.4). Joyce picked us up and took us to the Comfort Inn.

On Friday, Lance, Joyce's husband, picked us up at the Comfort Inn, dropped us at PA 501 (mm 1193.4), and took our backpacks on to the barbershop near the Union House B&B in Port Clinton. The trail actually comes within a block of the barbershop and Union

Princess and Angel Mary (shuttle driver in the Duncannon, Pennsylvania, area).

House. The barber likes hikers and had agreed to hold our packs until we got there. The Union House only opens on the weekends and doesn't open until 5 p.m., so they suggested that we leave our packs with the barbershop. We hiked 24.1 miles from PA 501 (mm 1193.4) to Port Clinton, Pennsylvania (mm 1217.5). We stopped by the barbershop and retrieved our packs. They offered us donuts and coffee/sodas. The post office was across the street, so I took the opportunity to mail a few items home (maps that I had already used).

We were able to check into the Union House B&B around 5 p.m. It was a unique experience. The place was an old house with many antiques. Apparently, it housed Union soldiers during the war. It had a shared bath with one toilet and one clawfoot bathtub. It was a

Rocketman and Princess enjoying an early breakfast at the Filbert Bed & Breakfast in Danielsville, Pennsylvania.

positive experience. Plus, there was a washer and dryer in the basement that I used. The restaurant was filled with antiques as well. We sat at the bar and later learned that the bartender was the cook and the owner. He was great. We also enjoyed some of his fine wine with a delicious dinner. We told him what we were doing, and he offered to make us a sandwich that evening for breakfast the next morning since we were leaving early. Plus, we left our packs on the front porch for the Carlin's to pick up the next morning and move on to our next destination— Blue Mountain Summit on PA 309.

On Saturday, we hiked 26.3 miles from Port Clinton, Pennsylvania, (mm 1217.5) to PA 309 (mm 1243.8). The Blue Mountain Summit B&B is located on PA 309 a few hundred feet west of the AT. Kenny is the owner and says he doesn't like hikers, but he really does. He has a nice restaurant and bar and three nice rooms with private baths. We stayed there last year and enjoyed it.

We had already called Kathy at the Filbert B&B for reservations and shuttles for the next three days. We stayed there last year and knew we wanted to stay there again. Kathy's place is extremely clean and has all the fine touches. She offers breakfast early if you prefer. Plus, she'll shuttle you anywhere and almost anytime.

On Sunday, we hiked 8.3 miles from PA 309 (mm 1243.8) to Lehigh Furnace Gap, Ashfield Road (mm 1252.1). Kathy picked up our packs from the Blue Mountain Summit and picked us up at Lehigh Furnace Gap. We cleaned up, and she did our laundry. There aren't any places to walk to for food, but there are a couple of places that will deliver food, so we ordered out. Kathy has a shed, where she prefers that you leave your packs and boots. She also has clean loaner clothes for you to use while she washes your clothes. This also ensures that her place stays clean, which it does. Again, a very nice and clean place to stay.

On Monday, we decided to jump ahead because it was going to rain and we wanted to avoid climbing the rock

*Princess making it up the pile of rocks at
Lehigh Gap to the Palmerton Superfund site
located in Palmerton, Pennsylvania.*

Princess with Kathy—the shuttler and owner of the
Filbert Bed & Breakfast in Danielsville, Pennsylvania.

pile at Lehigh Gap just before the Super Fund in the rain.
We hiked 15.4 miles from Little Gap Road (mm 1262.4)
to PA 33, Wind Gap (mm 1277.8). Kathy dropped us off
and picked us up.

On Tuesday, we hiked 10.3 miles from Lehigh
Furnace Gap (mm 1252.1) to Little Gap Road (mm
1262.4). We made it up the pile of rocks just before the
rain. Kathy dropped us off and picked us up.

In the meantime, we called ahead for reservations for
three nights at the Deer Head Inn in Delaware Water Gap.
The Deer Head Inn opens for dinner on Thursday–Saturday
evenings, and they have jazz on Friday and Saturday evenings.
The owners are big jazz fans and one actually plays, so they
know the performers and are able to attract some real talent.

Last year, we passed through Delaware Water Gap on Monday and Tuesday so we missed the jazz.

On Wednesday, Kathy dropped us off at PA 33, Wind Gap (mm 1277.8) and took our packs on to the Deer Head Inn. We hiked 15.6 miles to PA 611, Delaware Water Gap (mm 1293.4). The Deer Head Inn is located right off the trail as you enter Delaware Water Gap. We were able to check in, get cleaned up, and grab a bite at the Village Farmer bakery. The bakery has a number of tasty items. We bought our breakfast for the next day there. Later, we had dinner at the Sycamore Grill, which was extremely good as well. The only advertised place to do laundry was at the Pocono Inn. If you are willing to ask around, you may get lucky to find other places.

Princess and Professor T outside the Deer Head Inn in Delaware Water Gap, Pennsylvania.

Delaware Water Gap (mm 1277.8) to
Bear Mountain Bridge, Ft. Montgomery (mm 1403.6)
125.8 miles

The only two places that advertised shuttle service in the Delaware Water Gap area were the Edge of the Woods Outfitters and the Water Gap Adventures. I called both places—one didn't have the time, and the other was extremely expensive and didn't want to pick us up until 8 a.m. In 2014, we went to the Church of the Mountain hostel, which is located next to the Deer Head Inn and someone there shuttled us. So we headed back there, and sure enough, we were able to find a kind gentleman (Kenny) that agreed to shuttle us the next three days at any time.

On Thursday, Kenny picked us up at 6 a.m. sharp from the Deer Head Inn and shuttled us to Millbrook—Blairstown Road (mm 1307.4), and we hiked SOBO 14 miles back to the Deer Head Inn. After cleaning up and doing our laundry, we enjoyed a fabulous dinner at the Deer Head Inn.

On Friday, Kenny picked us up at 6 a.m. again and shuttled us to US 206, Culvers Gap (mm 1321.8), and we hiked SOBO 14.4 miles back to Millbrook—Blairstown Road (mm 1307.4). Later, he picked us up at Millbrook—Blairstown Road and shuttled us back to the Deer Head Inn. We were able to enjoy dinner again and the jazz that evening was truly a treat worth coming back for.

We called ahead to the High Point Country Inn for reservations for the next two nights. We stayed there last year and enjoyed our time with the manager, Ron, and his dog, Murph.

On Saturday, Kenny picked us up at 6 a.m. again. He took us to US 206, Culvers Gap (mm 1321.8) and took our packs onto the High Point Country Inn. We hiked 14.3 miles to NJ 23, Port Jervis, New York (mm 1336.1), where we called Ron and he picked us up.

The High Point Country Inn is a motel, and it's clean. Ron does your laundry for a modest fee, and he'll shuttle you fairly early each morning. There are no restaurants within walking distance, but there are a couple of places that will deliver meals. We enjoy it there.

On Sunday, Ron shuttled us to Liberty Corners Road (mm 1349.7), and we hiked 13.7 miles back to NJ 23 (mm 1336.1) where Ron picked us up.

We called ahead to Anton's on the Lake and made reservations with Matt for the next three nights. We stayed there last year and wanted to return. They have a washer/ dryer that you can use, and there are several nice places to eat/ drink within walking distance. Plus, Matt provides you with shuttle service as part of your stay if you stay several nights.

On Monday, Ron shuttled us back to Liberty Corners Road (mm 1349.7) and took our backpacks onto Anton's. We hiked 12.4 miles to Warwick Turnpike (mm 1362.2) where Matt picked us up and took us back to Anton's in Greenwood Lake, New York.

On Tuesday, Matt dropped us off at Warwick Turnpike (mm 1362.2), and we hiked 13.1 miles to Lakes Road (mm 1375.3) where he picked us up.

On Wednesday, Matt dropped us off at Lake Road, and we hiked 13.9 miles to Arden Valley Road (mm 1389.2). We walked down the hill to the Tiorati Circle where we waited for Matt to pick us up.

We called ahead to the Bear Mountain Bridge Motel for reservations for one night. They only shuttle to/from the

*The High Point Country Inn off Route 23 North
in Wantage, New Jersey.*

*trailhead to their motel. We stayed there last year. We also
stayed at the Holiday Inn Express last year because they have
coin laundry, but they don't provide shuttle service. It's about
a two-mile walk from the trailhead to the motel. The BBQ
place across the street from the Bear Mountain was great for
dinner, and the bagel café was good for breakfast.*

On Thursday, Matt dropped us off at Arden Valley
Road (mm 1389.2) and took our packs on to the Bear
Mountain Bridge Motel in Ft. Montgomery. We hiked
14.4 miles to the Bear Mountain Bridge (mm 1403.6)
where the owner of the Bear Mountain Bridge Motel
picked us up.

Bear Mountain Bridge, Ft. Montgomery (mm 1403.6) to
Guilder Pond (mm 1512.6)
109.0 miles
*In 2014, we had difficulty finding someone to shuttle us
from Ft. Montgomery, New York, to Wingdale, New York.
We got lucky this year with Martin "The Edge" Hunley.*

Even though he had to work, he was willing to pick us up before he went to work and after he got off. He knew the trailheads, and he actually maintained one of the shelters. He agreed to shuttle us from Ft. Montgomery (mm 1403.6) to Wingdale (mm 1448.7).

We called ahead to the Dutchess Motor Lodge in Wingdale, New York, for reservations for three nights. We stayed there last year. Although the rooms weren't the best, they were better than anything else we saw along the way. About a half a mile down the road was the best BBQ in New York, so we were good with our stay.

(In 2016, we did not stay at the Dutchess Motor Lodge. Since we had our car, we chose a place in Cold Spring called the Pig Hill B&B for one night and another place in Hopewell Junction the next night

Princess at the 911 Memorial Flag painted atop the Shenandoah Mountain in New York.

called Le Chambord. Both were very nice with good food options.)

On Friday, the owner of the Bear Mountain Bridge Motel took us to the Bear Mountain Bridge (mm 1403.6), and we hiked 14.5 miles to Dennytown Road. Originally, we had planned to hike further, but the weather was humid and we just ran out of energy. We had made backup plans with Martin and called him to let him know that we could only make it to Dennytown Road. Martin picked up our backpacks at the Bear Mountain Bridge Motel and then us at Dennytown Road and took us to the Duchess Motor Lodge.

On Saturday, the owner of Duchess (Bill) dropped us off at NY 22 (mm 1448.4), and we hiked 14.5 miles SOBO to NY 52 (mm 1433.9) where Martin picked us up.

On Sunday, Martin picked us up at the Dutchess, took us to NY 52 (mm 1433.9) and later picked us up at

Bear Mountain Bridge Motel in Fort Montgomery, New York.

Dennytown Road (mm 1433.9). We hiked SOBO 15.8 miles while Martin worked.

We called ahead to Cooper Creek B&B for a one-night reservation and pick up/drop off at the trailhead. Cooper (the owner) also agreed to pick up our backpacks from the Duchess for a fee. We also called ahead to the Bearded Woods for a four-night reservation and backpack pickup at Cooper Creek.

On Monday, Martin picked us up at the Dutchess before work and took us to NY 22 (mm 1448.4). We hiked 18.7 miles to CT 341, Schaghticoke Road (mm 1467.1) where Cooper picked us up.

This was our first time to stay at the Cooper Creek B&B in Kent, Connecticut. Last year (2014), we stayed at the Fife 'n Drum Inn. It was very nice, but they didn't provide a shuttle service, so we went to Cooper Creek. Cooper was fabulous. He took us back into town so we

Rocketman and Martin "The Edge" Hunley (shuttle driver in the Hopewell Junction area) at the Dutchess Motor Lodge in Wingdale, New York.

Princess in front of the Fife 'n Drum home where
we stayed in a nice room off the back porch.
Located in Kent, Connecticut.

could do laundry and get dinner. We ate at the Fife 'n Drum Restaurant, and it was outstanding. The Cooper Creek B&B was another historic home. The bathrooms had been upgraded, so it was extremely nice. Cooper was willing to get up early the next morning and provide us with breakfast and a ride back to the trailhead.

On Tuesday, Cooper took us back to the trailhead. We hiked 15.9 miles from CT 341, Schaghticoke Road (mm 1467.1) to W. Cornwall Road (mm 1483.0) where Hudson, owner of the Bearded Woods Bunk and Dine, picked us up. He had already picked up our backpacks from the Cooper Creek B&B earlier that day.

We stayed at the Bearded Woods with Hudson and Big Lu last year and loved it. Hudson fixed up his

One of the two bunkrooms inside the Bearded Woods
Bunk and Dine in Sharon, Connecticut.

basement to house up to nine people comfortably. It's extremely clean. We share a bathroom, but again, Big Lu keeps it spotless. Big Lu cooks a gourmet dinner and breakfast as part of your stay. They do your laundry. Hudson/Big Lu shuttles to W. Cornwall and Salisbury as part of your stay. It's the best! The only drawback is that you are in a bunkroom. There is one double bed for couples, but it's not private.

On Wednesday, we hiked 16.2 miles from W. Cornwall Road (mm 1483.0) to Salisbury (mm 1499.2) where we walked into town, grabbed a bite at the Country Bistro, picked up a few items at the LaBonne's Market, and waited for Hudson to shuttle us back to the Bearded Woods.

On Thursday, we took a much needed zero day. At this point, we had another hiker (Spartacus) that wanted to join us slack packing. He had completed roughly 1,500 miles carrying his pack, and he was beaten down. He had lost thirty-five pounds and was ready for something different. We welcomed him.

On Friday, Hudson took us (including Spartacus) to Guilder Pond, Massachusetts, Everett Road (mm 1512.6), and we hiked 13.4 miles back to Salisbury (mm 1499.2). Spartacus loved the hike with us. He liked hiking faster without many breaks until the end of the day.

Guilder Pond (mm 1512.6) to Williamstown (mm 1592.6)
80.0 miles

We called ahead to Jess Treat for a three-night reservation at her house. Jess will shuttle, do your laundry, cook breakfast,

Hudson and Big Lu—owners and hosts of the Bearded Woods Bunk and Dine in Sharon, Connecticut.

and take you to a nearby restaurant. She enjoys hikers, is fun, and just interesting to talk with. She's a writer and has published a few short stories.

On Saturday, Hudson took us back to Guilder Pond (mm 1512.6) and took our backpacks onto Jess's place. We hiked 16.8 miles to MA 23 (mm 1529.4) where Jess picked us up. At this point, we picked up another hiker that wanted to slack pack with us, Focus. We welcomed Focus. The only concern I had was that my brother planned to join us in New Hampshire, and I didn't know if a party of five would be a problem with shuttles and accommodations. We let both Spartacus and Focus know

Left to right: Focus, Cookie Lady aka Marilyn Wiley, Princess, Roy, Cookie Lady's husband, and Spartacus at the home of the Cookie Lady just 100 yards off of the Washington Mountain Road trailhead in Becket, Massachusetts.

of our concerns, and we all agreed that we would work it out later.

On Sunday, Jess took us to Goose Pond Road (mm 1545.8), and we hiked 16.4 miles back to MA 23 (mm 1529.4) where Jess picked us up.

On Monday, Jess took us back to Goose Pond Road (mm 1545.8), and we hiked 13.8 miles to Washington Mountain Road (mm 1559.6) where we walked east to visit the Cookie Lady for some cookies while we waited for Jess to pick us up.

We called ahead to the Shamrock Village Inn for a one-night reservation. We stayed here last year. The Inn is a

Left to right: Focus, Jess Treat (shuttle driver and rents rooms in her Sheffield home), Princess, and Spartacus at trailhead near Great Barrington, Massachusetts.

half-block from the trail and is near a decent restaurant/ bar and bakery. The rooms are decent as well. We also called the Bascom Lodge for a one-night reservation on top of Mount Greylock for Wednesday night.

On Tuesday, Jess took us back to Washington Mountain Road (mm 1559.6) and our backpacks on to the Shamrock Village Inn in Dalton. We hiked 10.5 miles to Gulf Road/High Street, Dalton, Massachusetts, (mm 1570.1) and then to the Shamrock Village Inn.

On Wednesday, Spartacus planned to hike with his daughter, so we left our backpacks with him, so his wife could shuttle them to our next destination, which was the Bascom Lodge on top of Mt. Greylock. Focus, my husband, and I left early that morning and hiked 16.2 miles to the top of Mt. Greylock (mm 1586.3). The Bascom Lodge was nice. They did have running hot water. They also have several private rooms, but they go quickly. Although we had made reservations, they managed to overbook, and we had to share a room with Focus, but that was better than the bunkroom. They served breakfast and dinner at the lodge. The dinner was extremely nice and the rooms were clean. I would stay there again, even though they did make an error in our reservations.

We called ahead to the Williamstown Motel for a one-night reservation. We stayed here last year. The rooms are clean, and they will do your laundry. There are several places within walking distance to eat and get supplies.

On Thursday, we left Mt. Greylock (mm 1586.3) and hiked a short 6.3 miles to MA 2, Hoosic River (mm 1592.6) where we called the Williamstown Motel to be picked up. Spartacus's wife shuttled our packs from the Bascom Lodge to the Williamstown Motel.

We called ahead for reservations at the Autumn Inn in Bennington, Vermont, for one-night. We also called David Ackerson to shuttle our backpacks from the Williamstown Motel to the Autumn Inn while we hiked. We also called ahead to the Green Mountain House for a four-night reservation, but Jeff would only allow us a three-night stay because he likes to give other hiker's an opportunity to experience his place. His place is nice, but it is more like a hostel than an inn, in that it has bunkrooms and shared bathrooms. We were able to get a private room with two twin beds. Jeff keeps the place clean, and he will shuttle you into town for resupply and meals. However, he will not shuttle you to/from the trailhead. He expects you to hitch into town where he will pick you up. I had problems with that, so we just hired a shuttle driver (John Perkins).

Williamstown (mm 1592.6) to Norwich, Vermont (mm 1745.6)
153.0 miles

On Friday, Spartacus's wife, Janelle, took us to the trailhead at MA 2, Hoosic River (mm 1592.6), and we hiked 18.4 miles to VT 9, Bennington, Vermont (mm 1611.0). The owner of the Autumn Inn picked us up at VT 9 and took us to the Autumn Inn. This establishment is one of the few that will pick you up at the trailhead. It's not the best place to stay because it's not that clean. They do have coin laundry service, and it is within walking distance to several nice restaurants.

We contacted John Perkins to take our backpacks from the Autumn Inn to the Green Mountain House and to shuttle us to and from the trailhead for the next few days.

On Saturday, John picked us and our packs up at the Autumn Inn. He took us to the trailhead at VT 9 (mm 1611.0), and we hiked 22.6 miles to Stratton-Arlington Road, Manchester Center, Vermont, (mm 1633.6) where he picked us up and took us to the Green Mountain House.

On Sunday, we took a zero day. The Green Mountain House is a house with three bedrooms upstairs and two full baths. Jeff, the owner, actually stays in a separate house next door but frequently visits to ensure we all understand

Outside of the Green Mountain House in Manchester Center, Vermont. Left to right: Focus, Spartacus, Princess, and Jeff, the owner of the Green Mountain House.

the rules, and he enjoys talking with all the hikers. The house has a nice washer and dryer. On the first floor, there's a full kitchen, dining room, half bath, and living room area that the guest may use. Spartacus made us breakfast each morning with blueberry pancakes, bacon, and maple syrup.

Since we could only stay three days at the Green Mountain House, we needed to move on north. We contacted the Silas Griffin B&B and made a two-night reservation. Kathy, the owner, said she would shuttle us for a fee.

On Monday, John Perkins took us back to Stratton-Arlington Road (mm 1633.6), and we hiked 17.5 miles to VT 11 & 30 (mm 1651.1) where he picked us up and took us back to the Green Mountain House.

On Tuesday, John Perkins took us back to VT 11 & 30 (mm 1651.1) and our backpacks onto the Silas Griffin B&B. We hiked 17.6 miles to Danby-Landgrove Road (mm 1668.7) where Kathy picked us up. Our cell service was sketchy at the pickup point. There was a big rock near the privy that you could stand on and get minimal service, as I had to call Kathy to let her know when we arrived. (When the shuttle driver is waiting on a cell phone call, it's important to find out from the driver where cell service is available, e.g., at the big rock. And, it's a good idea to have a Plan B in case cell service doesn't work. For example, if there is no call by a specific time, then come to pick us up regardless.)

The Silas B&B was a historical building. It looked very nice from the road but up close, it needed a lot of work. The rooms were nice and comfortable. Kathy did our laundry for $20, which was the highest that we had to pay on our entire trip. Breakfast was served from 7 to 11 a.m. Kathy did everything. She was the cook, shuttler, washer, etc.

We called ahead to the Long Trail Inn for a four-night reservation. We got two rooms that shared a bathroom in the middle. We had asked about shuttling, but they said they needed to know the details much earlier to schedule the shuttlers. However, they did give me several other people's contact information for shuttling. One was "Plans Too Much." Since I plan a lot, I contacted him. He had hiked the AT some time ago and knew the trail well. He was willing to support us all the way to New Hampshire. We were set for the next few days.

On Wednesday, we decided to eat Kathy's breakfast, which meant we had to wait until after breakfast to hit the trail. We didn't hit the trail until almost noon, which

Spectacular view from the Killington Peak Lodge located 0.2 miles east from the Cooper Lodge Shelter.

meant we got finished later than usual. Kathy took us to VT 103 (mm 1683.5), and we hiked 14.8 miles SOBO back to Danby–Landgrove Road (mm 1668.7) where she picked us up. We got cleaned up, and Kathy took us back to Sal's for dinner. She also did our laundry while we enjoyed dinner.

On Thursday, Kathy took us back to VT 103 (mm 1683.5). On the way, we left our packs in the red train at Qu's Whistle Stop. Plans Too Much had suggested that we leave our packs there, and his wife would pick them up and take them to the Long Trail Inn. He had good connections with the owner. We hiked 11.1 miles to Killington Peak Lodge (mm 1694.6). We took the blue blaze trail up to the ski lodge, which was fabulous. It was a nice, clear day, and the views were spectacular. The lodge was a restaurant—no lodging. We ate a nice lunch and enjoyed some fine wine. We took the gondola down, where we took a public bus that took us to the Long Trail Inn. (Plans Too Much told us about the bus, so we got a free ride to the inn.)

When we arrived at the inn, we picked up our packs and checked in. The inn has an Irish Pub associated with it with great food and Guinness on draft—a great place to stay for four nights. It also has a washer/dryer for the guests and a restaurant in addition to the pub.

On Friday, we took a side trail from the inn (Sherburne Pass Trail) to the AT and hiked 8.3 miles (mm 1702.8) back up to Killington Peak Lodge (mm 1694.6), then took the blue blazed back to the ski lodge where we had lunch again. We took the gondola back down and the bus back to the inn. (My brother was joining us in New

Hampshire, and we needed to slow down to meet him there. Hence the shorter mileages.)

We called ahead and made a two-night reservation at the Norwich Inn, New Hampshire. My brother was scheduled to meet us there, and we were going to take another zero day there.

On Saturday, Plans Too Much picked us up at the inn and shuttled us to Chateauguay Road (mm 1715.4). We hiked 12.6 miles SOBO back to Sherburne Pass Trail (mm 1702.8) and took it back to the inn.

On Sunday, Plans Too Much took us back to Chateauguay Road (mm 1715.4), and we hiked 12.9 miles to Pomfret Road (mm 1728.3) where he picked us up.

On Monday, Plans Too Much took us back to Pomfret Road (mm 1728.3) and took our backpacks on to Norwich Inn. We hiked 17.3 miles to Main Street (mm 1745.6) and then another block to the Norwich Inn. Norwich is the last town in Vermont on the AT. The Norwich Inn includes a nice restaurant and bar. It's also a microbrewery. We stayed here last year and liked the rooms, food, and microbrews. They have everything you need, except laundry service. And, there's no laundry service within walking distance, so I just washed our things in the sink and hung them up outside to dry.

Norwich, Vermont (mm 1745.6) to US 2, Gorham, New Hampshire (mm 1875.7) 130.1 miles

We called ahead and made a two-night reservation for the Dowd's B&B. The staff was friendly and said they could accommodate our shuttle requests because they were slow during the few days that we would be there. (Once we got there, we realized how lucky we were to catch them on a "slow" few days.)

On Tuesday, we took a zero, and my brother, Ranger, arrived to join us the rest of the way.

On Wednesday, we made arrangements to leave our backpacks in the lobby for Patrick of Dowd's B&B to pick up and take to the B&B while we hiked. My brother wanted to sleep in the woods as much as possible, so we marked his pack with instructions to Patrick to bring his pack when he picked us up. We left the Norwich Inn early that morning (mm 1745.6) and hiked 19.0 miles to Grafton Turnpike (mm 1764.6) where Patrick picked us up, gave my brother his backpack, and took the rest of us to the B&B. My brother stayed and camped in the woods. I took his dirty clothes to wash with ours, his daypack, and extra food with me.

Princess and Focus in front of the Dowd's Country Inn Bed and Breakfast in Lyme, New Hampshire.

This B&B was one of the nicest places we had stayed. We had private bathrooms, and they let us use their washer/dryer for our clothes. Next door was a general store that had freshly prepared food, beer, and wine. Next door, in the other direction, was a nice Italian restaurant. My job for my brother was to let him stay in the woods at night and slack with us during the day. So I kept any extra weight with us, so he only had what he needed each night brought to him at the end of the day and picked up in the morning when we arrived at the trailhead. We always decided ahead of time what time we would be back at the trailhead the next morning, so he could give his pack to the shuttle driver while we all hiked during the day. He called this a "hybrid" slack packing hike.

On Thursday morning, Patrick had agreed to serve us breakfast at 6 a.m. and take us to the trailhead afterward. Breakfast was made to order and delicious. Spartacus ran to the corner store and got himself and Ranger a homemade sandwich for lunch. Patrick took us back to the trailhead at Grafton Turnpike (mm 1764.6). We gave my brother his clean hiking clothes and exchanged his backpack for his daypack with fresh water in his bladder and lunch from Spartacus. He changed in less than two minutes and loaded his gear into Patrick's SUV to bring back at the end of the day. We hiked 16.1 miles to NH 25A (mm 1780.7) where Patrick picked us up and my brother retrieved his backpack, so he could camp again.

We called ahead to the Hiker's Welcome Hostel and made arrangements for Patrick to drop off our packs while we hiked to the hostel. We weren't sure about the next few days and how to work slacking the White Mountains. Last year, Rocketman supported me during this section, so we didn't have any experience on shuttles in this area.

On Friday morning, Patrick served us breakfast again and took us to the trailhead. Spartacus picked up lunch again for him and Ranger at the corner store, and he got Ranger a milkshake. Patrick drove us to NH 25A, Wentworth (mm 1780.7), and we hiked 9.8 miles to NH 25, Oliverian Brook (mm 1790.5). Patrick took our backpacks on to the Hiker's Welcome Hostel. We walked from the trailhead at NH 25 to the hostel. Spartacus had made arrangements with longtime friends who lived in New Hampshire (Rick and Penny) to pick us up and take us to his place for the evening. It was lovely. They made fresh pizzas and salads.

Rocketman and Princess climbing up to Moosilauke Mountain from the north side from Kinsman Notch to Oliverian Brook, NH25 near Glencliff, New Hampshire.

On Saturday morning, Rick let us drive one of his cars to the trailhead. We started at Lost River Road, NH 112, Kinsman Notch (mm 1799.8) and hiked 9.3 miles SOBO to NH 25, Oliverian Brook (mm 1790.5). We walked back to the Hiker's Welcome Hostel where we picked up our packs. This section is the beginning of climbing again—the Whites!

I had a friend from my working days that contacted me about being at a conference in the area and wanted to meet up with us. We made arrangements for her to pick us up at the Hiker's Welcome Hostel and take us to North Woodstock, New Hampshire. We had dinner at the Woodstock Inn. There were no rooms available at the Woodstock Inn, so we stayed at the Carriage Motel. We were able to make a two-night reservation at the Woodstock Inn for Sunday and Monday. Spartacus had a son who was working and going to school in the area, so he went with his son. His son wanted to hike Kinsman with us the next day.

I started working the Whites. I knew that I had to tent a section last year. It was 27.7 miles from Franconia Notch (mm 1816.1) to Crawford Notch, US 302 (mm 1843.8). The Appalachian Mountain Club has huts throughout the White Mountains and they have centers at some of the notches. The huts serve breakfast and dinner and have bunks and restrooms. They do not have showers or laundry facilities. The centers serve breakfast, lunch, and dinner. They have bunks and private rooms with hot showers. They do not have laundry facilities.

Galehead Hut was about halfway between Franconia and Crawford Notch, so I contacted them ahead of time to see what was available. There was one night with five vacancies, so I took it. We would need to take two zero days before we could stay at Galehead, so we needed to find a place in North Woodstock. (I should have worked this section earlier, but I just didn't know how much we could do. Both Rocketman and I were getting tired and needed to rest. The others didn't seem to need the rest. The Appalachian Mountain Club's Highland Center was located near Crawford Notch, so I also called them for a room. I was able to reserve a private room, and Focus reserved a bunk. My brother chose to tent nearby and Spartacus decided to stay with his friend Rick.

The Woodstock Inn does not offer shuttle service to/from the trailhead, but the Gale River Motel did. I talked with Kevin, the Gale River Motel owner, and he agreed to take us to the trailhead and then take our backpacks on to the Appalachian Mountain Club's Highland Center at Crawford Notch. I made arrangements with the Highland Center to accept our packs from Kevin before we left. This was tricky as we were having our packs shuttled forward while we spent a night in a hut in the Whites.

On Sunday, we made arrangements with the management at Carriage Motel to leave our backpacks with them while we hiked that day. The Woodstock Inn was a half mile up the road, and they didn't have a place to hold our backpacks. Spartacus's son picked us up at the Carriage Motel and drove us to the Kinsman Notch trailhead on Lost River Road, NH 112 (mm 1799.8). We hiked 16.3 miles to Franconia Notch (mm 1816.1) where we had made arrangements with The Connection to pick us up and take us to the Woodstock Inn. We got the driver to stop at the Carriage Motel, so we could retrieve our backpacks and take them with us to the Woodstock Inn.

On Monday, we took a zero day at the Woodstock Inn. We stayed here last year. It's a great place. The restaurant is nice, and they brew their own beer. They don't have laundry facilities, but there is a laundromat within walking distance.

On Tuesday, Kevin from the Gale River Motel picked us up from the Woodstock Inn and took us to

June 9, 2016: Rocketman and Princess being rescued by the New Hampshire Fish and Game's Specialized Search and Rescue Team. Assisting were Androscoggin Valley Search and Rescue (AVSAR) and Pemigewasset Valley Search and Rescue (PEMI).

his place. He did provide laundry service, so we did our laundry. We took another zero day and walked to a local restaurant for dinner that evening. There really wasn't much in the area, and the service at the local restaurant was deplorable.

On Wednesday, Kevin drove us to Franconia Notch (mm 1816.1). We hiked 13 miles to the Frost Trail to the Galehead Hut (mm 1829.1). This hut was very nice with four bunk rooms stacked three bunks high. I was lucky enough to get a bottom bunk. The food was good, and it was nice to have drinking water available for our water bottles.

In 2016, this section is where we got in trouble. We checked the local weather and the Appalachian Trail Conservancy weather for the Galehead Hut. The forecast was 40 to 55 degrees with a 20 percent chance of rain. When we were halfway across the Franconia Ridge, above the tree line, we were exposed to 50 mph sustained winds, driving sleet, and 80–90 mph gusts. My glasses iced over and I couldn't see. I could no longer discern the trail after passing over Mt. Lafayette. Although we were only 0.2 miles from the tree line, we didn't know it and couldn't see where to go. Ultimately, we had to use our DeLorme inReach and set off the SOS signal. We were lucky that another hiker (Wolfman) came by and helped us to a location behind a large rock outcropping. He set up his tent around us and covered us with his sleeping quilt until the Search and Rescue (SAR) team reached us.

We were later informed that we should have checked the Mount Washington weather site for climbs over 4,000 feet, which predicted exactly what we were experiencing.

In particular, go to the Mount Washington Observatory website at www.mountwashington.org. Under the menu, select "Experience the Weather," then select "Higher Summits Forecast" for the above 4,000-foot weather forecast.

On Thursday, we headed out after breakfast and hiked 14.7 miles to Crawford Notch, US 302 (mm 1843.8). Actually, we took a side trail to the Highland Center because it was a 3+ mile walk along US 302 to the center. Our backpacks were at the center waiting on us.

The next section of the Whites was also challenging. We knew we could hike from Crawford Notch to Mt. Washington in a day. Then from Mt. Washington to Pinkham Notch in a day. Both would be difficult but doable. There is an auto road up Mt. Washington, and

Entrance into the Appalachian Mountain Club's Highland Center Lodge located at Crawford Notch in New Hampshire.

there are shuttles. There are time restrictions on the shuttles, and they will not wait on you. If the weather turns bad, you could be stranded. The last shuttle is at 4 p.m., and we knew we should make it there with time to spare if all went well. We made arrangements to leave our backpacks at the Highland Center, and Dan from Trail Angels would pick them up and take them to the White Mountain Lodge in Gorham. The Highland Center staff advised us to fasten a nametag on our backpacks to be sure they could be identified. We made arrangements with Marney, the owner of the White Mountain Lodge, for three nights and shuttles to/from the trailhead. She knew that we planned to hike up Mt. Washington and take a shuttle down where she would pick us up and take us to her place—White Mountain Lodge.

There was another section of the Whites that was challenging. Last year (2014), I hiked 21.1 miles from Pinkham Notch to Gorham. This year I thought it best to break this up into two sections, so Rocketman and I decided to do that. I checked the Carter Notch Hut, and they did have space, so we made reservations for us to stay there. Focus and Spartacus decided to hike this 21.1-mile section in a day. My brother actually decided to just spend two nights out in the woods.

On Friday, we ate breakfast at the Highland Center, left our backpacks behind the check-in counter, and hiked 12.5 miles to Mount Washington (mm 1856.3). We took the Mt. Washington Auto Road shuttle down to their visitor center, and Marney's shuttle was waiting for our arrival. Later, Dan from Trail Angels arrived at Marney's—but with only ONE backpack. He said that they could only find one backpack behind the counter. He said he tried to call, but there was no signal. He was willing to drive me back to the Highland Center to find the other backpacks. It took over an hour of driving to get to the center. I went to the counter, and they had no idea where our backpacks were. They sent me to the basement where they store backpacks for guests. There must have been fifty packs stored in the basement. I found ours and retrieved them. Anyway, this is a lesson learned. This place is huge. Many people work here, and they change shifts. I didn't recognize anyone from the day before or the morning. I'm not sure how you could guarantee that your backpacks could be picked up by a total stranger.

On Saturday, we were to take the shuttle back up to Mt. Washington and hike 13.5 miles to NH 16, Pinkham

*White Mountain Lodge and Hostel
in Gorham, New Hampshire.*

Rocketman in front of the Lake of the Clouds Hut on top Mount Washington, New Hampshire.

Spartacus and Focus waiting to ride down the Mount Washington Auto Road in the Mt. Washington Stagecoach.

Notch (mm 1869.8) where Marney's shuttle would take us back to the White Mountain Lodge.

Marney's place was nice. She has bunks and private rooms. She also provided laundry service and breakfast. Plus, they shuttled you into town for dinner and supplies as needed.

On Sunday, we headed back to Pinkham Notch (mm 1869.8). Rocketman and I hiked 5.9 miles up the Wild Cats to the Nineteen Mile Brook Trail—Carter Moriah Trail to Carter Notch Hut (mm 1875.7) where we were staying the night. Spartacus and Focus were moving on to Gorham and then taking a zero. My brother moved on to camp in the woods. He would meet us at Marney's

Left to right: Focus, Princess, Ranger, Honey, Bear, and Spartacus planning our next few days of hiking at The Cabin. Honey and Bear own the cabin and provide shuttle service to and from the trail in Andover, Maine.

the next day. We actually enjoyed this hut. It was older and had several smaller huts with bunks. Our room had two sets of bunks, and we had it to ourselves and could spread out. The meals were good and the people were nice.

US 2, Gorham, New Hampshire (mm 1875.7) to Long Falls Dam Road (mm 2020.5)
144.8 miles

On Monday, after breakfast, we hiked 15.2 miles from mm 1875.7 to US 2, Gorham (mm 1890.9). Marney's place is located on US 2 along the trail. It was great!

The 31.1-mile section from US 2, Gorham, New Hampshire, (mm 1890.9) to Grafton Notch, Maine, (mm 1922.0) took me two days last year. Plus, this section has Mahoosic Notch, which is a one-mile stretch through a giant rock pile with gaps and crawls. I did not know how we were going to slack pack this section, but I was told by Homer, one of our shuttle drivers back in Virginia, that he and his family had slacked this section years ago when they thru-hiked. He told me to contact Earl at The Cabin.

I had been talking with Earl at The Cabin on and off for a couple of weeks about the five of us staying with him and slacking the section between Gorham, New Hampshire, and Rangeley, Maine. Although we were out of the Whites, we were approaching Mahoosic Notch— one of the most challenging sections on the trail. Earl suggested that we take a zero before doing Mahoosic Notch to ensure we were rested and the weather was forecasted to be nice that day. The Cabin had one private room, so Rocketman and I took that.

On Tuesday, Spartacus picked us up in his truck, and we headed to The Cabin to meet Earl and Margie (Bear and Honey). He met with us to find out what our needs were and was good with us starting out early each day. He agreed to serve us breakfast at 5 a.m. and leave for the trail at 6 a.m. every morning. (Also, from this point on, we had Spartacus's truck that we could use for runs into town, pick up points, etc. He lived a couple of hours from the trail at this point.)

On Wednesday, after an early, hearty breakfast, we left in two trucks. We dropped Spartacus's truck at our end point—Grafton Notch, ME 26 (mm 1922.0). Then Earl drove us down a gravel road to a side (access) trail that would lead us to the AT (mm 1913.8) Mahoosic Notch. The side trail was the Mahoosic Notch side trail and was about two miles. We hiked 8.2 miles NOBO on the AT to Grafton Notch, where Spartacus's truck was waiting on us.

On Thursday, Earl drove us back to the Mahoosic Notch side trail, and we hiked the two miles back to the AT and headed SOBO. We hiked 10.3 miles to Gentian Pond Shelter (mm 1902.7). From the shelter, we took another two-mile side trail (Austin Brooke Trail) to a side road where Earl was waiting to pick us up.

On Friday, we took two trucks again. We dropped Spartacus's truck back at the side road near the Austin Brooke Trail, and then Earl took us onto US 2, Gorham, New Hampshire (mm 1890.9). We hiked 11.8 miles to the Gentian Pond Shelter (mm 1902.7). From the shelter, we took the Austin Brooke Trail back down to the side road where we had left Spartacus's truck.

On Saturday, we took two trucks again. Earl took us to Grafton Notch, ME 26 (mm 1922.0), and we hiked 10.3 miles to East B Hill Road (mm 1932.3). Hopper (a helper to Earl) had taken Spartacus's truck to our end point and left it for us.

On Sunday, we took two trucks again. Earl took us to East B Hill Road (mm 1932.3), and we hiked 10.1 miles to South Arm Road (mm 1942.4). Hopper had taken Spartacus's truck to our end point again.

Ranger, Focus, Rocketman, and Spartacus at the New Hampshire–Maine State Line on the AT.

On Monday, we took two trucks again. Earl took us to South Arm Road (mm 1942.4), and we hiked 13.2 miles to ME 17, Oquossoc (mm 1955.6). Hopper had taken Spartacus's truck to our end point again.

The Cabin was great. They had a washer and dryer that we could use. They served breakfast and dinner except on Saturday nights. The private room was in the main house, and you shared their very large and nice bathroom and laundry room. They had a hostel in the basement with bunks, a living room area, bathroom, washer/dryer, and kitchen. They also had several pop-up campers with beds. Focus, Spartacus, and Ranger took one each. Both Honey and Bear loved hikers. They loved hiking themselves, and it was such a treat being a part of their lives for a week. They must have enjoyed us as they decided to have a "steak and lobster" night while we were there. So Sunday night, we all enjoyed fresh Maine lobsters and steak. It was certainly a nice treat.

I called ahead to the Farmhouse and made a two-night reservation and shuttle service. We stayed at the Farmhouse

The Farmhouse Inn in Rangeley, Maine. A hostel and private rooms catering to AT hikers and friends of hikers.

last year (2014) and really liked the owners—Shane and Stacy. They have a couple of private rooms with baths, so we rented them.

On Tuesday, we took both trucks again. Earl dropped us at ME 17, Oquossoc (mm 1955.6) and took our packs on to the Farmhouse. Hopper took Spartacus's truck to ME 4, Rangeley (mm 1968.8). We hiked 13.2 miles to ME 4 and took the truck to the Farmhouse.

On Wednesday, we dropped Spartacus's truck at ME 4 and Shane took us onto Woods Road (mm 1982.3). We hiked SOBO 13.5 miles back to ME 4, Rangeley (mm 1968.8). We took Spartacus's truck back to the Farmhouse.

The next section was either 10.4 or 18.7 miles. Rocketman and I decided to break it up into two sections. Spartacus and Focus did it in one day (Thursday) and then they drove to Spartacus' cabin on the lake in Maine and took a zero day on Friday.

I had called Susan at the Stratton Motel for a three-night reservation and shuttle service. The motel was clean but needed some TLC. We found out that Susan was selling her place to Shane and Stacy at the end of the month, so hopefully, Shane will be able to give it a facelift. Stratton had a small convenient store, laundromat, and restaurant within walking distance of the motel.

On Thursday, Shane took Rocketman and me back to Woods Road (mm 1982.3) and took our backpacks on to the Stratton Motel. We hiked 10.4 miles to Caribou Valley Road (mm 1992.7) where Susan from the Stratton Motel picked us up and took us to the motel.

On Friday, Susan took us back to Caribou Valley Road (mm 1992.7), and we hiked 8.3 miles to ME 27 (mm 2001.0). Susan picked us up and took us back to the motel where Spartacus and Focus rejoined us.

I called ahead to the Sterling Inn (near Caratunk, Maine) for a reservation and shuttle service. Sterling provided laundry service, had private rooms, provided breakfast and lunch, and provided shuttle service to the local restaurant. They also had a small resupply service.

Last year, it was difficult slacking the portion between Caratunk and Monson because of the lack of roads. The distance worked out to be either 10 or 20 plus miles each day. At this point, we were both tired so 10-mile hikes seemed reasonable. However, my brother and Focus weren't worn down like we were, so I felt like we were holding them back. Not a good feeling.

I called ahead to Shaw's in Monson about reservations and shuttles. I had talked with them previously because they work with the AT Lodge in Millinocket to slack you through the 100-mile Wilderness. Last year (2014), we camped in the wilderness and realized that you could slack it with all the logging roads running through it. The Shaw's used Dawn and her team for their shuttles, so I talked with her about slacking us from Moxie Pond to halfway through the wilderness.

On Saturday, we decided to do a "key swap" with Spartacus and Focus. (A key swap is where one group would be dropped off at the start of the trailhead and the other group would drive to the end and start hiking towards the first group. When we pass each other, the first group takes the key to the car and hikes to the car. Then we drive to the start and pick up the other group. We had

Rocketman approaching the plank to cross
the Carrabessett River near Stratton, Maine.

to do this the last half of the wilderness because the AT Lodge had not scheduled us.) Susan took Rocketman and me back to ME 27 (mm 2001.0), and we hiked 19.5 miles to Long Falls Dam Road (mm 2020.5) where Spartacus left his truck. We took his truck back to the hotel and Rocketman went back to ME 27 to pick up Spartacus and Focus. Unfortunately, Spartacus took a bad fall, and it took him much longer to finish this hike, so Rocketman waited longer than usual on his arrival at the trailhead. We had severe rain, lightning, and hail that day.

Long Falls Dam Road (mm 2020.5) to
100-mile Wilderness (mm 2074.7)
54.2 miles

On Sunday, Susan took us back to Long Falls Dam Road (mm 2020.5), and Spartacus took our packs on to Sterling's. We planned another "key swap" that day. We hiked 17.5 miles to US 201, Caratunk (mm 2038.0). However, when we met up with Focus, he informed us that Spartacus couldn't hike and was waiting for us at US 201. This section has the canoe ride across the river, so we had to wait until 1 p.m. for the canoe. Once we crossed the river, we found Spartacus in the parking lot waiting for us in his truck. He took us to check-in at Sterling's. It was a horrible evening, as Spartacus had decided that he needed to come off the trail for a few days to let his bionic knee recover.

Fording in Maine.
Left to right: Ranger, Pintsize, and Princess.

On Monday, Sterling dropped us at Moxie Pond South (mm 2049.9), and we hiked 11.9 miles SOBO back to US 201, Caratunk. We walked to a telephone and called Sterling for a pickup. Our cell phones did not work, but you could walk about a half mile to a public phone. Once we cleaned up, Sterling took us onto Shaw's in Monson.

On Tuesday, Dawn and Gary shuttled us to Bald Mountain Road (mm 2060.7), and we hiked 10.8 miles SOBO back to Moxie Pond South (mm 2049.9). Gary picked us up and took us back to Shaw's.

On Wednesday, Dawn shuttled us to Bald Mountain Road (mm 2060.7), and we hiked 14 miles to ME 15, Monson (mm 2074.7). Shaw's picked us up at ME 15 and took us back to their place.

There are really not a lot of choices in Monson. Shaw's had several rooms, a private room, a bunk room, two full bathrooms and a half bath, and laundry. They

Shaw's Hiker Hostel on the edge of the
100-mile Wilderness in Monson, Maine.

served breakfast every day and dinner on Monday nights because the restaurants downtown are closed.

I had called ahead to the AT Lodge and talked with OldMan several times about slacking services needed and room reservations. We had agreed with Dawn and OldMan that we would switch from Dawn to OldMan on Sunday near the halfway point of the wilderness.

A happy-face blaze!

100-mile Wilderness (mm 2074.7) to
Mount Katahdin (mm 2189.2)
114.5 miles

We entered the 100-mile Wilderness on Thursday. Dawn shuttled us the Otter Pond parking. We took a blue-blazed trail 0.8 miles to the AT (mm 2090.0). We hiked 15.3 miles SOBO back to ME 15 (mm 2074.7) where Shaw's picked us up and took us back to the lodge.

On Friday, Dawn shuttled us back to the Otter Pond parking lot. Again, we took the 0.8-mile trail to the AT (mm 2090.0) and hiked 14.5 miles to Katahdin Ironworks Road (mm 2104.5). Dawn's husband Dick picked us up.

On Saturday, Dick shuttled us back to Katahdin Ironworks Road (mm 2104.5), and we hiked 14.9 miles to Logan Brook Road (mm 2119.4) where he picked us up again.

I called the OldMan and one of his workers had no record of my reservations for a room nor shuttles. He said they were booked up for Sunday and could not help. They did say they could help accommodate us on Monday but the shuttles weren't guaranteed. Fortunately for us, Spartacus called and said he was ready to come back, so he said he would pick us up on Sunday and join us on Monday for the hike to Katahdin.

On Sunday, Dawn dropped us off at Logan Brook Road (mm 2119.4) and took our backpacks on to the AT Lodge. We hiked 13.7 miles to Jo-Mary Road (mm 2133.1) where Spartacus was waiting to pick us up. It was a great day to have our friend rejoin us! We drove into Millinocket to the AT Lodge, and they said they didn't have enough room for all of us, so we picked up our backpacks and moved into the Katahdin Inn. The AT Lodge did have room to accommodate us the next three nights, so we took the reservations. We canceled the shuttles and decided to "key swap" the rest of the way using Spartacus' truck.

On Monday, we hiked 22.5 miles from Jo-Mary Road (mm 2133.1) to Pollywog Stream (mm 2156.6).

On Tuesday, we hiked 17.5 miles from Pollywog Stream (mm 2156.6) to Abol Bridge (mm 2174.1).

On Wednesday, we hiked 9.9 miles from Abol Bridge (mm 2174.1) to Katahdin Stream Campground (mm 2184.0).

Thursday was the big day! We all got to hike together again because you climb 5.2 miles up to Katahdin and return. We hiked 5.2 miles from Katahdin Stream Campground (mm 2184.0) to the top of Katahdin (mm 2189.2) and back down. Note: the AT ends at the top of Mt. Katahdin, so the 5-mile hike down from the top is just extra miles.

We had a beautiful day to hike up to Mt. Katahdin. Left to Right: Rocketman, Spartacus, Princess, Ranger, and Focus

Special Sections

The Great Smoky Mountains National Park

You have to spend the night in the Smokies! The total distance is 70.5 miles (mm 167.4 to mm 237.9). We divided this stretch into two sections: 1) From the Fontana Dam Visitor Center to Newfound Gap, US 441 (39.7 miles) and 2) from Newfound Gap to Green Corner Road (33.5 miles). The northern boundary of the Smokies ends at mm 237.9 TN 32, NC 284, Davenport Gap, but we hike another 2.7 miles to Green Corner Road (mm 240.6) to stay at the Standing Bear Farm.

After Fontana Dam Visitor Center (mm 166.3), we entered the Great Smoky Mountains National Park (mm 167.4). You will need a permit and to pay a backcountry

Pay and print a permit up to thirty days in advance at smokiespermits.nps.gov/ index.cfm?BCPermitTypeID=1 fee while hiking through this 70.5-mile section. There is an online system that allows you to pay and print a permit up to thirty days in advance (smokiespermits.nps.gov/index.cfm?BCPermitTypeID=1).

A great place to register and print your permit is at the Nantahala Outdoor Center (NOC) outfitter at mile marker (mm) 137.3, US 19 & 74 before you reach the Smokies.

While hiking the Smokies, you will have to stay in their shelters. It's my understanding that there are four slots for thru-hikers in each shelter. This is important because the other slots are sold and reserved online and if it is full and there are four thru-hikers already in the shelter, you can be bumped out. So you have to carry a tent just in case the shelters are full unless you can reserve a spot in all the shelters ahead of time. Plus, the rules state that you can only tent if the shelter is full. During the times that we have hiked the Smokies, it was the same time as the college spring break period so the shelters have been full of students on spring break. Plan accordingly. The only road that you will cross in the Smokies is Newfound Gap, US 441, at mm 207.1. (The same road goes up to the Clingmans Dome parking lot and at mm 199.1 there is a trail 0.5E to the parking lot but it is not open until April 1. Plus this really only buys you 8.2 miles so you still need to tent unless you can hike 40 miles in one day with lots of ups and downs on rocky terrain.)

We entered the Smokies with our full backpacks knowing that we would tent two nights before coming off at Newfound Gap to stay in Gatlinburg, Tennessee. Our first section to Newfound Gap was 41 miles because we started at the Fontana Dam Visitor Center, which was a 1-mile hike to the Smokies southern boundary. The first day we hiked 13.5 miles and stayed at the Russell Field Shelter. The second day we hiked 16.7 miles and stayed at the Double Spring Gap Shelter. The third day we hiked 10.8 miles to Newfound Gap where my brother's wife was parked to give us a ride into Gatlinburg.

We stayed at the Grand Prix Motel mainly because it was in Gatlinburg and easy to walk to places to eat. Plus, they had a coin washer and dryer machine, which most of the hotels didn't have or advertise. The previous year, we stayed at the Days Inn and had to take Gatlinburg's transit system to a laundromat and the total trip time was around three hours. That was not worth our time. Although the Grand Prix needed a face-lift, it was tolerable and the people were nice. They also provided a shuttle back to Newfound Gap for $30. We took two days off just to rest up.

The second section of the Smokies was 33.5 miles, so we decided we would spend another night in the woods and break this up into two days. (If you do the math, this section of the Smokies is only 30.8 miles not 33.5 but we knew we wanted to stay at the Standing Bear Farm so we hiked the additional 2.7 miles.) The first day we hiked 15.6 miles and stayed at the Tri-Corner Knob Shelter. The next day, we hiked 17.9 miles to mm 240.6 at Green Corner Road and stayed in a suite at the Standing Bear Farm.

Last year, we stayed in the cabin, which was nice. They built a small room (called a suite) overlooking a small creek on their property, and we stayed in it. It was not completely finished and had room for a double bed. Although we prefer staying in the cabin, it has three beds, so they would prefer renting it to a family or small group instead of just one couple. According to AWOL's *AT Guide* book, there was another place to stay, but we stayed here last year and thought it was okay and liked the people. Plus, they do shuttles early in the morning. One drawback is laundry. They only have a scrub board (instead of a washer), but they do have a dryer that you can use. They also have a small room with a kitchen and a fairly well-stocked resupply so you can cook yourself meals. And they also have a hostel and a tree house with a futon. They have a crude shower house and a composted privy. In 2016, they updated their privy to a port-a-john.

We stayed two nights at the Standing Bear mainly because of their shuttle service.

Shenandoah National Park (SNP)

The total trail miles through the SNP is 103.2 miles (from mm 862.3 to mm 865.5). The only road through the SNP is Skyland Drive, and shuttle drivers typically live in the valleys on either side of the park, so the shuttles get expensive, and it takes time to get to the trailhead. However, the AT crosses Skyland Drive many times so there are plenty of access points to the trail. There is a list of shuttle drivers posted on the roadside railing as you reach Rockfish Gap (mm 861.7). Call them and let them know your plans. You will most likely have to use several different drivers because the drive to and from any point along Skyland Drive takes considerable time and can be expensive. There are four access points to Skyland Drive—the south end, the north end, US 211 (Luray), and US 33 (Swift Run Gap). We like staying at the Skyland Lodge because the rooms are clean and the restaurant/bar is very good. However, there are no laundry services at Skyland. There are three other places in SNP that do have coin laundry: Loft Mountain Campground, Lewis Mountain Campground, and Big Meadows Campground.

White Mountain National Forest

You can slack most of the Whites by staying several nights at the AMC (Appalachian Mountain Club) Huts. We spent the night at two huts (Galehead and Carter) and the Highland Center. Otherwise, we arranged shuttles at road crossings and stayed in motels or hostels. Another alternative is to go from hut to hut. The huts are nice, but they have no showers and no laundry. They do have pillows and a blanket, but you should take your sleeping bag or liner. You can also buy energy bars, etc., so you don't have to carry extra food. You can refill your water bottles, and they provide breakfast and dinner if you have a reservation. You can also purchase hot drinks and soup.

The Whites are tough hiking, and you are above tree line many times. Make sure you look at the weather for Mount Washington including predictions for the weather above the tree line. We got in trouble on Mount Lafayette in 2016 and had to be rescued. We looked at the local weather and the ATC weather forecast for where we had planned to stay, Galehead Hut, but failed to check on weather above 4,000 ft. using the Mt. Washington weather site. Use the website at: Mount Washington Observatory | Higher Summits Forecast.

www.mountwashington.org/experience-the-weather/higher-summit-forecast.aspx

We did stay at the Highland Center at Crawford Notch. This is a very nice AMC lodge with a bunkroom and several private rooms with private baths. The only issue we had was with our backpacks. The taxi we hired to pick up our backpacks only picked up one pack because the staff had taken the other packs to the basement for storage. The cab driver had no idea which packs were ours. You really need to talk with someone at the front desk about this to make sure your packs can be identified. The cell service in this area was bad, so the driver could not get in touch with us.

There is a shuttle service that runs between the visitor center at the base of Mount Washington and the visitor center at the top of the mountain. We took it up and down Mt. Washington. You need to make sure that you can hike from the AMC Highland Center to the top of Mt. Washington before 4:30 p.m. when the last shuttle departs from the top of the mountain. This should not be a problem if you leave the Highland Center early enough. And when you continue NOBO, you should take the first shuttle from the visitor center at the base to the top of Mt. Washington to give you enough time to hike 13.5 miles from the top of Mt. Washington to Pinkham Notch. This was the most difficult hike for me because of the miles of rock hopping down from Mt. Madison.

Mahoosuc Notch

The owners (Honey and Bear) of The Cabin in Andover, Maine, will slack you from Gorham to Rangeley. You will have to use two 2-mile side trails to get you to/from the AT trail, but it's worth it. The Cabin does have one private room in the main part of the house. They also have a hostel with bunks and several pop-up campers.

Kennebec River

You must take the ATC-sponsored canoe across the Kennebec River (mm 2037.5) in Caratunk, Maine, so you need to make sure you know the schedule. (The canoe shuttle is the only way to get across the Kennebec River that is approved by the ATC.) When we hiked in 2015, the canoe was available for a two-hour period twice a day: 9–11 a.m. and 2–4 p.m. In 2016, it was 9 a.m. to 2 p.m. Check the ATC website for information (appalachiantrail.org). Go to Explore the Trail and then Trail Updates for Maine.

appalachiantrail.org/home/
explore-the-trail/explore-by-state/Maine

For us, this section was a 17.5-mile hike with the Kennebec River crossing near the end of the hike (mm

2020.4, Long Falls Dam Road to mm 2037.9, US 201, Caratunk, Maine). So, you'll need to start early to ensure you get there before 2 p.m. We got there around 1 p.m. with a 7 a.m. start. This section was relatively easy compared to most other sections in Maine.

100-mile Wilderness

You can slack the entire 100-mile Wilderness. The 100-mile Wilderness starts in Monson, Maine, at mm 2074.6, ME 15. There is an AT Visitor Center in Monson where you can pre-register for the required AT long-distance hiker permit to enter Baxter State Park and summit Katahdin.

We worked with the owners of Shaw's Lodging in Monson from Moxie Pond at the south end near mm 2049.8 to halfway through the wilderness. They had an agreement with the previous owners of Shaw's for the shuttle service. You should know that the shuttles through the wilderness are expensive because of limited access and fees to enter the logging roads. The commute to and from the trailhead alone was at least an hour drive one-way. Shaw's shuttled us over halfway through the wilderness and did a great job.

There was one section that we had to take an unnamed side trail in to hit the AT, but they knew exactly how to describe what we had to do. Then we were to be handed off to the owners of the AT Lodge in Millinocket. (The owner of Shaw's is related to the owners of the AT Lodge, so I thought the handoff would go smoothly. It did not!) When we were ready for the handoff, the AT Lodge had failed to record our reservations and said they were booked up. Fortunately, we were able to find alternative lodging in Millinocket. And we were lucky with shuttling because a member of our group lived in Maine and had his truck, so we were able to do a "key swap."

Baxter Park

A free AT long distance hiker permit is required of all northbound long distance hikers who enter Baxter State Park. Southbound hikers are not required to have a permit but must follow existing regulations. Permits can be obtained at Baxter State Park Headquarters and Katahdin Stream Campground. Pre-registration for AT long distance hiker permits can be obtained at the AT Visitor Center in Monson, Maine.

If you work with the AT Lodge, they will shuttle you to and from Baxter State Park for your summit. Otherwise, if you have family/friends that plan to summit with you, you will need to obtain a car pass to enter the park and park at the Katahdin Stream Campground while you hike. The car pass can be obtained online at baxterstateparkauthority.com under day parking reservations.

baxterstateparkauthority.com/
reservation/parkingReservations.htm

Glossary

Trail Names (as they appear)

Rocketman: co-author, Greg Reck, spouse to Princess aka Lelia Vann

Ranger: Princess aka Lelia's brother

Princess: co-author, Lelia Vann, spouse to Rocketman aka Greg Reck

AWOL: David Miller, author of the AT Guide book

Maverick: thru-hiker we met on the trail and at the Cantarroso Farm in Erwin, Tennessee

Wye Knot: thru-hiker staying at Cantarroso Farm in Erwin, Tennessee

10-K: shuttle driver in Erwin, Tennessee

Route Step: thru-hiker we met on the trail

Boss: trail boss for thru-hiker Pintsize

Pintsize: thru-hiker we met on the trail

Runaway: thru-hiker we met in Damascus, Virginia

Grasshopper: thru-hiker we met in Damascus, Virginia

Coffee Grounds: past thru-hiker that provides Trail Magic along the AT during March/April starting in Georgia

Mister Gizmo: shuttle driver in Waynesboro, Virginia, and Shenandoah National Park area

Lady Moose: thru-hiker we met in Waynesboro, Virginia, and again at the Terrapin Station Hostel.

Angel Mary: shuttle driver in Duncannon, Pennsylvania

Professor T: thru-hiker we met on the trail and later decided to slack pack with us in Delaware Water Gap, Pennsylvania.

The Edge: Martin Hunley, shuttle driver for the Hopewell Junction, New York, area and trail maintainer.

Hudson and Big Lu: owners of the Bearded Woods Bunk and Dine in Sharon, Connecticut

Spartacus: a thru-hiker that joined us at Bearded Woods

Focus: a thru-hiker that joined us after Bearded Woods

Cookie Lady: Marilyn Wiley, met just off Washington Mountain Road trailhead in Becket, Massachusetts

Plans Too Much: shuttle driver in Killington, Vermont

Wolfman: Adam DeWolfe, AT hiker that rescued us on June 9, 2016, on the Franconia Ridge in the New Hampshire Whites.

Honey and Bear: Margie and Earl, owners of The Cabin in Andover, Maine

Hopper: AT thru-hiker that helps Honey and Bear at The Cabin during hiking season.

OldMan: owner of the AT Lodge in Millinocket, Maine

Appendix I
Draft AT Plan
2015

Note: Page numbers in parentheses refer to the
AWOL's *AT Guide*

Map 1: 0-80 miles

Day 1–2/28   12.3 miles
0.0   Springer
12.3   Cooper Gap USS 15, 42, 80
R.E. & Gay's

Day 2–3/1   8.5 miles
12.3   Cooper Gap
17.2   Gooch Gap USFS 42 gravel

20.8   Woody Gap, GA 60
R.E. & Gay's

DAY 3–3/2   **10.9** MILES
20.8   Woody Gap
31.7   Neel Gap, US19
R.E. & Gay's

DAY 4–3/3   **6.9** MILES
31.7   Neel Gap, US19
37.7   Tesnatee Gap
38.6   Hogpen Gap, GA 348
Helen, GA

DAY 5–3/4   **14.3** MILES
38.6   Hogpen Gap, GA 348
52.9   Unicoi Gap, GA 75, Helen, GA
Helen, GA

DAY 6–3/5   **16.7** MILES
52.9   Unicoi Gap, GA 75, Helen, GA
69.6   Dicks Creek Gap, US 76, Hiawassee, GA
R.E. & Gay's

Map 2: 80–184 miles

DAY 7–3/6   **16.7** MILES
69.6   Dicks Creek Gap, US 76, Hiawassee, GA
86.3   Standing Indian Shelter
TENTING

DAY 8–3/7   20.4 MILES
86.3   Standing Indian Shelter
100.3   Albert Mtn. bypass, west 0.2 to parking on USFS 67
106.7   Wallace Gap, W. Old Murphy Rd., Franklin, NC
Cabin

DAY 9–3/8   9.0 MILES
106.7   Wallace Gap, W. Old Murphy Rd., Franklin, NC (p. 17)
115.7   Wayah Gap, Wayah Rd.
Cabin

DAY 10–3/9   13.5 MILES
115.7   Wayah Gap, Wayah Rd.
129.2   Tellico Gap, NC 1365 (p. 20)
Cabin

DAY 11–3/10   8.1 MILES
129.2   Tellico Gap, NC 1365 (p. 20)
137.3   NOC, US 19&74 (p. 20)
Fryemont Inn

DAY 12–3/11   13.4 MILES
137.3   NOC, US 19&74 (p. 20)
150.7   Stecoah Gap, NC 143
Fryemont Inn

DAY 13–3/12   14 MILES
150.7   Stecoah Gap, NC 143

164.7   Fontana Dam, NC 28 (p. 22)
Fryemont Inn

SMOKIES…Map 3: 167–238 miles

Day 14–3/13   15.1 miles
164.7   Fontana Dam, NC 28 (p. 22)
177.0   Mollies Ridge Shelter (12 spaces)
179.8   Russell Field Shelter (14 spaces)

Day 15–3/14   16.7 miles
179.8   Russell Field Shelter (14 spaces)
182.7   Spence Field Shelter (12 spaces)
196.5   Double Spring Gap (12 spaces)

Day 16–3/15   10.8 miles
196.5   Double Spring Gap (12 spaces)
207.3   Newfound Gap, US 441, Gatlinburg, TN
Meet Alan
Stay at Days Inn 865-436-5811. No laundry but should be able to use Grand Prix Motel coin laundry
Or
Grand Prix Motel 865-436-4561 $39 has coin laundry
Allows pets:
Motel 6. 865-436-7813
Microtel. 865-436-0107

Day 17–3/16   ZERO Monday

Day 18–3/17 Tuesday   15.6 miles
207.3   Newfound Gap, US 441, Gatlinburg, TN
222.9   Tri-Corner Knob Shelter (12 spaces)

DAY 19–3/18   18.4 MILES

222.9   Tri-Corner Knob Shelter (12 spaces)

241.3   Green Corner Rd. (p. 29); Standing Bear
         Hostel; private cabin: 423-487-0014

Begin Map 4: 238 - 352 miles

DAY 20–3/19   18.7 MILES

241.3   Green Corner Rd. (p. 29)

253.9   SR 1182, Max Patch Rd. (p. 30)

260.0   Lemon Gap, NC 1182, TN 107

DAY 21–3/20   14.8 MILES

260.0   Lemon Gap, NC 1182, TN 107

274.8   NC 209 + US 25/70, French Broad River, Hot
         Springs, NC

p. 33 Creekside Court 828-215-1261 $75 D lower
weekdays. Three nights total.
Maildrop and shuttles:
Bluff Mtn. Outfitters: 828-622-7162
152 Bridge St., Hot Springs, NC 28743

DAY 22–3/21   ZERO SATURDAY

DAY 23–3/22   14.4 MILES
SOBO BACK TO HOT SPRINGS

274.8   NC 209 + US 25/70, French Broad River, Hot
         Springs, NC

289.2   NC 208, TN 70, Allen Gap (p. 34)

DAY 24/25–3/23   10.8 OR 19.2 MILES

289.2   NC 208, TN 70, Allen Gap

310.0   Devil Fork Gap, NC 212
318.4   Sams Gap, US 23, I-26 (p. 35)
Move onto Erwin–Cantarroso Farm

Day 26–3/25   13.4 or 24.5 miles
318.4   Sams Gap, US 23, I-26 (p. 35)
331.8   Spivey Gap, US 19W (p. 38)
342.9   River Rd., Erwin, TN
Cantarroso Farm 423-833-7514 will shuttle
Maildrop: 777 Bailey Lane, Erwin, TN 37650
Private Suite $90
10-K (Tom and Marie) shuttle: 423-330-7416

Begin Map 5: 352–469 miles

Day 27–3/26   8.4, 11.8, or 20.2 miles
SOBO back to Cantarroso Farm
342.9   River Rd., Erwin, TN
351.3   Indian Grave Gap, TN 395
354.7   Beauty Spot Gap, trail parallel to USFS 230
        from here north to Deep Gap (p. 39)
363.1   Iron Mtn. Gap, TN 107, NC 226

Day 28–3/27   9.3 or 15.9 miles
363.1   Iron Mtn. Gap, TN 107, NC 226
372.4   Hughes Gap, TN 1330, Hughes Gap Rd.
379.0   Carver Gap, TN143, NC 261
Move onto Mtn. Harbour B&B: 866-772-9494 (p. 42)

Day 29–3/28   14.8 miles
379.0   Carver Gap, TN143, NC 261
393.8   US 19E Elk Park, NC

Mtn. Harbour B&B
866-772-9494
Maildrop: 9151 Hwy 19E, Roan Mtn., TN 37687

DAY 30–3/29   10.4 MILES
SOBO BACK TO MT. HARBOUR B&B
393.8   US 19E Elk Park, NC
404.2   Walnut Mtn. Rd. (p. 41)

DAY 31–3/30   14.3 MILES
404.2   Walnut Mtn. Rd. (p. 41)
418.5   Dennis Cove Rd., USFS 50 (p. 44)
Black Bear Resort (p. 47)
423-725-5988
Maildrop: 1511 Dennis Cove Rd., Hampton, TN 37658

DAY 32–3/31   13 MILES
SOBO BACK TO BLACK BEAR RESORT
418.5   Dennis Cove Rd., USFS 50 (p. 44)
431.5   Wilbur Dam Rd. (p. 45)

DAY 33–4/1   16.1 MILES
431.5   Wilbur Dam Rd.
447.6   TN 91, Shady Valley, TN (p. 48)
2.5 E Switchback Creek Campground: 407-484-3388
2-person cabin $40. Showers, Laundry. Call for ride. (p. 47)
We did not stay here because they would not shuttle us back to the trail until after 9 a.m. Instead, we moved onto Damascus, VA.

DAY 34–4/2   21.2 MILES

447.6   TN 91, Shady Valley, TN

468.8   Damascus (p. 49)

Lazy Fox—Ms. Ginny: 276-475-5838

Maildrop: 133 Imboden St., Damascus, VA 24236

Call Mt. Rogers–they may pick up packs at Switchback
Creek and take to Ms. Ginny's.

Mt. Rogers Outfitter for shuttle: 276-475-5416

Begin Map 6: 469–562 miles

DAY 35–4/3   ZERO

DAY 36–4/4   17.2 OR 18.5 MILES

SOBO BACK TO LAZY FOX

468.8   Damascus

486.0   US 58, footbridge, stream

487.3   VA 601, Beech Mtn. Rd.

DAY 37–4/5   18.4 OR 22.9 MILES

BACK TO LAZY FOX

487.3   VA 601, Beech Mtn. Rd.

505.7   The Scales (p. 52)

510.2   Fox Creek, VA 603 (p. 53)

DAY 38–4/6   13.6, 21.4, OR 22.1 MILES

(FROM MAP VA 622 LOOKS CLOSER TO ATKINS. ASK SKIP)

510.2   Fox Creek, VA 603 (p. 53)

523.8   VA 670, South Fork, Holston River

531.6   VA 16 (p. 53) Mt. Rogers Visitor Center

532.3   VA 622 (p. 54)

Comfort Inn 276-783-2144

Maildrop: 5558 Lee Hwy, Atkins, VA 24311
Skip: 276-783-3604
Bubba: 276-266-6147 barnes.james43@yahoo.com

DAY 39–4/7   10.4 MILES
532.3   VA 622 (p. 54)
542.7   VA 683, US11, I-81, Atkins
Back to Comfort Inn 276-783-2144
Maildrop: 5558 Lee Hwy, Atkins, VA 24311

Begin Map 7: 551–636 miles

DAY 40–4/8   14.9 MILES
542.7   VA 683, US11, I-81, Atkins
554.9   VA 42 (p. 55), O'Lystery Pavilion
Comfort Inn again

DAY 41–4/9   17.7 MILES
554.9   VA 42 (p. 55)
572.6   VA 623 (p. 58)
Comfort Inn again

DAY 42–4/10   19.4 MILES
572.6   VA 623 (p. 58)
591.0   Northend of VA 612, I-77
Comfort Inn again

DAY 43–4/11   17.6 MILES
591.0   Northend of VA 612, I-77
608.6   VA 606 Trent's Grocery (pp. 60 & 62)
276-928-1349 Shuttle, shower, laundry. Call for a private room.

Otherwise, call Don Raines 540-921-7433 for shuttle to Woods Hole

Day 44—4/12   15.2 MILES
608.6   VA 606 Trent's Grocery (p. 60)
623.8   Sugar Run Gap. Sugar Run Rd. (gravel), road
         fork in view to east Woods Hole Hostel (.5E)

Woods Hole: 540-921-3444 Neville & Michael
Maildrop: Woods Hole Hostel
3696 Sugar Run Rd., Pearisburg, VA 24134
Private room: $55
Don Raines 540-921-7433 for shuttle

Begin Map 8: 632–745 miles

Day 45—4/13   12 MILES
623.8   Sugar Run Gap.
635.8   US 460, Senator Shumate Bridge, New River,
         Circle under north end of bridge

MacArthur Inn
540-726-7510 Call for ride in Pearisburg area trailheads,
ride $5 each way.
Don Raines 540-921-7433 for shuttle

Day 46—4/14   18.9 MILES
SOBO BACK TO MACARTHUR?
635.8   US 460
654.7   Stony Creek Valley, 0.1 to parking on VA 635

Day 47—4/15   13.2 OR 20.6 MILES
654.7   Stony Creek Valley, VA 635
667.9   VA 632, cross Johns Creek on Footbridge

675.3   Footbridge, Sinking Creek, VA 42 (p. 68)

Trail "east" here is compass west. 1W Sublett Place 540-544-3099. Home and cottage for rent. Will they pick up? Call ahead and ask.

If not, other shuttles:

Joe Mitchell 540-309-8615 Four Pines

Homer Watcher 540-266-4849

Del Schechterly 540-529-6028

We ended up using Homer Witcher. He was fantastic. We moved onto Daleville, VA. We stayed 1 night at the HOJO and then several nights at the Super 8.

Day 48–4/16   11.4 miles
SOBO?

675.3   Footbridge, Sinking Creek, VA 42 (p. 68)

686.7   VA 621, Craig Creek Rd.—Maybe SOBO if
         Sublett will shuttle.

Day 49–4/17   17 miles
SOBO Dragon's Tooth

686.7   VA 621, Craig Creek Rd. (p. 65)

694.1   VA 620 (gravel), footbridge, Trout Creek

702.1   VA 624, Newport Rd. (Close to Four Pines
         Hostel)

703.7   VA 785, Blacksburg Rd.

Four Pines: Joe Mitchell 540-309-8615

We did not stay at Four Pines. We stayed in Daleville at the HOJO for 1 night before we traveled home.

Day 50–4/18   24.1 miles

703.7   VA 785, Blacksburg Rd.

727.8   US 220, Daleville, VA (p. 67)
HOJO 540-992-1234
Maildrop: 437 Roanoke Rd., Daleville, VA 24083
Have Joe take our stuff to HOJO
Other shuttles:
Homer Witcher 540-266-4849
Del Schechterly 540-529-6028
Maybe travel home for tooth implant from here since we have access to rental cars.

Begin Map 9: 745–861 miles

DAY 51–4/19   16.1 OR 19.9 MILES
SOBO BACK TO HOJO
727.8   US 220, Daleville, VA (p. 67)
743.9   BRP 95.3, Harveys Knob Overlook
747.7   BRP 91.9, Mills Gap Overlook (p. 70)

DAY 52/53–4/20–21 ZERO TOOTH IMPLANT ON THE 21ST. GET OUR SUMMER GEAR FROM HOME.

DAY 54–4/22   8.3 OR 19.6 MILES
747.7   BRP 91.9, Mills Gap Overlook (p. 70)
756.0   VA 624, Jennings Creek (1.2 E Middle Creek
         CPG—will they pick us up @ USFC 812)
767.3   USFS 812 (Parkers Gap Rd.) 0.1N on AT,
         Apple Orchard Falls Trail
Middle Creek Campground. Cabins available sleeps 4-6.
Showers & Laundry.
540-254-2550–they say to ask about shuttles
See if they'll pick up. Otherwise Ken Wallace shuttle: 434-609-2704

We stayed in Daleville for several days before we moved onto Lexington, VA.

DAY 55–4/23   17.3 MILES
767.3   USFS 812 (Parkers Gap Rd.) 0.1N on AT (p. 71)
784.6   US 501, VA 130 (p. 75)
Lynchburg/Blue Ridge KOA cabins 4-person. Laundry & showers.
434-299-5228 (p. 72)
Maildrops: 6252 Elon Rd., Monroe, VA 24574
Ken Wallace shuttle: 434-609-2704

DAY 56–4/24   21.8 MILES
784.6   US 501, VA 130 (p. 75)
806.4   US 60, Buena Vista, VA
Maildrop:
502 S. Main B&B: 540-460-7353 (p.79)
Lexington, VA 24450
Call for pickup for $10 pp

DAY 57–4/25   16.3 OR 25.4 MILES
SOBO–THE PRIEST?
806.4   US 60, Buena Vista, VA
822.7   Spy Rock Rd. (formerly Fish Hatchery Rd. unpaved)
831.8   VA 56, Ty River suspension bridge (p. 77)
Stay back at 502 S Main B&B

DAY 58–4/26   15.5 MILES
831.8   VA 56, Ty River suspension bridge

847.3   Dripping Rock, BRP 9.6, spring
Stay in Waynesboro—Tree Streets Inn–have them pick us up at BRP 9.6

Begin Map 10: 861–906 miles

Day 59–4/27   14.4 miles
847.3   Dripping Rock, BRP 9.6, spring
861.7   US 250 Rockfish Gap, Waynesboro (p. 80)
Maildrop: (p. 82)
Tree Streets Inn: 540-949-4484 Call for pick up
421 Walnut Ave., Waynesboro, VA 22980

Day 60–4/28   19.9 miles
SOBO back to Rockfish Gap & Tree Streets Inn
861.7   US 250 Rockfish Gap, Waynesboro (p. 80)
881.6   Skyline 87.4, Black Rock Gap (p. 81)

Begin Map 11: 906–941 miles

Day 61–4/29   24.2 miles
881.6   Skyline 87.4, Black Rock Gap
905.8   Skyline 66.7
Either go back to Tree Streets Inn or stay at Skyland Resort
Skyland Resort 540-999-2212; Shuttle by Yellow Cab of Shenandoah 540-692-9200

Day 62–4/30   18.3 or 26.2 miles
905.8   Skyline 66.7
924.1   Big Meadows Wayside
932.0   Skyland Resort
Skyland Resort 540-999-2212

Begin Map 12: 941–970 miles

DAY 63–5/1   18.3 MILES
SOBO BACK TO SKYLAND RESORT?
932.0   Skyland Resort
950.3   Elkwallow Wayside (p. 90)

DAY 64–5/2   15.3 MILES
950.3   Elkwallow Wayside (p. 90)
965.6   Compton Gap Trail ("Chester Gap" post), (p. 91)

Front Royal Terrapin Station Hostel (p. 94); Mike Evans
540-539-0509
2-night special $50 includes slackpack
Maildrop: 304 Chester Gap Rd., Chester Gap, VA 22623

Begin Map 13: 970–1003 miles

DAY 65–5/3   20.2 MILES
SOBO BACK TO TERRAPIN STATION
965.6   Compton Gap Trail ("Chester Gap" post), (p.91)
985.8   Signal Knob, VA 638 (p. 92)

DAY 66–5/4   17.1 MILES
985.8   Signal Knob, VA 638
1002.9   Bears Den Rocks (p. 93)

Bears Den Hostel (p. 95)
540-554-8708
Call for private room and slacking.
Maildrop: Bears Den Hostel
18393 Blue Ridge Mountain Rd., Bluemont, VA 20135

Begin Map 14: 1003–1026 miles

DAY 67–5/5   20.5 MILES

1002.9   Bears Den Rocks (p. 93)

1023.4   High St., Harpers Ferry, WV (p. 96)

Town's Inn

304-932-0677

Maildrop: ATC HQ, 799 Washington St., Harpers Ferry, WV 25425

Begin Map 15: 1024–1064 miles

DAY 68–5/6   ZERO

DAY 69–5/7   17.5 MILES

SOBO BACK TO TOWN'S INN

1023.4   High St., Harpers Ferry, WV

1040.9   Turners Gap, US Alt 40 (p. 97)

DAY 70–5/8   13.4, 14.9, 17.5, OR 23.1 MILES

1040.9   Turners Gap, US Alt 40 (p. 97)

1054.3   Wolfsville Rd., MD 17

1055.8   Foxville Rd., MD 77

1058.4   Raven Rock Rd., MD 491

1064.0   Pen Mar County Park (p. 102)

Burgundy Lane B&B (p. 105)

717-762-8812

Free laundry & shuttle to trailhead. Longer for a fee. Maildrop: They may take our stuff onto Scottish Inn 128 W. Main St., Waynesboro, PA 17268

Begin Map 16: 1064–1082 miles

DAY 71–5/9   18.2 MILES

1064.0   Pen Mar County Park (p. 102)

1082.2   US 30 (p. 103)

Scottish Inn & Suites (p. 106) 717-352-2144, 800-251-1962

$69D will pickup/return for $5pp

Maildrop:

5651 Lincoln Way East

Fayetteville, PA 17222

We decided to spend extra days at the Burgundy Lane B&B in Waynesboro, PA, instead of moving to the Scottish Inn.

Begin Map 17: 1082–1112 miles

DAY 72–5/10   20.2 MILES

1082.2   US 30 (p. 103)

1102.0   Pine Grove Furnace SP

Ironmasters Mansion (p. 106)

717-486-4108 Call for private room. Last year the guy did shuttling.

Gary Grant Shuttle: 717-706-2578

Maybe call Holly Inn to see if they'll pick up/drop off to eat there.

Begin Map 18: 1112–1147 miles

DAY 73–5/11   19.3 MILES

1102.0   Pine Grove Furnace SP

1121.3   PA 174, Boiling Springs

Allenberry Resort Inn $40 D (p. 107)
800-430-5468
Maildrop:
1559 Boiling Spring Rd.
Boiling Springs, PA 17007
Allenberry Resort Inn is closed. In 2016, we stayed at a
B&B on the river in Boiling Springs.

DAY 74–5/12   16.5 MILES
1121.3   PA 174, Boiling Springs (p. 109)
1137.8   PA 850
Comfort Inn Riverfront, 525 S. Front St., Harrisburg, PA
17104
717-233-1611
Call Angel Mary for shuttle 717-834-4706

DAY 75–5/13   9.1 MILES
1137.8   PA 850 (p. 110)
1146.9   Duncannon, PA High St. & Broadway. Have a
         few beers at the Doyle!
Call Angel Mary 717-834-4706 for shuttle back to
Comfort Inn Riverfront

Begin Map 19: 1147–1182 miles

DAY 76–5/14   17.7 MILES
SOBO back to Duncannon
1146.9   Duncannon, PA High St. & Broadway
1164.6   PA 325, Clarks Creek north of road (p. 111)
Call Angel Mary to take us back to the hotel then to
trailhead & drop our bags to Days Inn, Licksdale.

DAY 77–5/15   17.4 MILES

1164.6   PA 325, Clarks Creek north of road (p. 111)
1182.0   Swatara Gap, PA 72, Licksdale, PA (p. 114)
Days Inn $55S (p. 116)
717-865-4064

Begin Map 20: 1182–1294 miles

DAY 78–5/16   11.4 MILES

1182.0   Swatara Gap, PA 72, Licksdale, PA (p. 114)
1193.4   PA 501–501 Shelter
Comfort Inn (Pilot Travel Center across the street has
laundry) (p. 116)
570-345-8031
Carlin's AT Shuttle: 570-345-0474

DAY 79–5/17   24.1 MILES

1193.4   PA 501–501 Shelter
1217.5   Port Clinton, PA (p. 118)
Union House B&B
610-562-3155
610-562-4076 after 5 p.m.

DAY 80–5/18   26.3 MILES

1217.5   Port Clinton, PA (p. 118)
1243.8   PA 309, on left
Blue Mtn. Summit (p. 122)
570-386-2003
Maildrop: 2520 W Penn Pike, Andreas, PA 18211

DAY 81–5/19   13.9 MILES

1243.8   PA 309, on left

1257.7   Superfund Trailhead (p. 124)
Filbert B&B (Kathy) (p. 126)
610-428-3300
Maildrop: 3740 Filbert Drive, Danielsville, PA 18038

DAY 82–5/20   20.1 MILES
SOBO BACK TO FILBERT?
1257.7   Superfund Trailhead (p. 124)
1277.8   PA33 Wind Gap (p. 125)

DAY 83–5/21   15.6 MILES
1277.8   PA33 Wind Gap (p. 125)
1293.4   PA 611 Delaware Water Gap
Deer Head Inn (p. 128)
570-424-2000
Maildrop: Edge of the Woods Outfitters
110 Main St., Delaware Water Gap, PA 18327

Begin Map 21: 1294–1372 miles

DAY 84–5/22   14 MILES
SOBO back to Delaware Water Gap
1293.4   PA 611 Delaware Water Gap (p. 125)
1307.4   Millbrook–Blairstown Rd. (p. 130)

DAY 85–5/23   14.4 MILES
1307.4   Millbrook–Blairstown Rd.
1321.8   US 206, Culvers Gap (p. 131)
Forest Motel (p. 129) $55D, laundry $20. Call for pickup.
Barbara 973-948-5456
We moved onto High Point Country Inn instead of
staying at the Forest Motel.

DAY 86–5/24   14.3 MILES
1321.8   US 206, Culvers Gap (p. 131)
1336.1   NJ 23, Port Jervis, NY (p. 131)
High Point Country Inn $80D Free pickup/return (p. 129)
973-702-1860
Maildrop: 1328 NJ 23, Wantage, NJ 07461

DAY 87–5/25   16.8 MILES
1336.1   NJ 23, Port Jervis, NY (p. 131)
1352.9   County Rd. 565, Glenwood, NJ (p. 132)
Appalachian Motel (p. 135)
973-764-6070 $70-110D. Call for ride.
Maildrop: 367 Rt 94, Vernon, NJ 07462
We stayed at High Point Country Inn instead of moving onto Appalachian Motel and we updated our maildrop to Anton on the Lake.

DAY 88–5/26   18.8 MILES
1352.9   County Rd. 565, Glenwood, NJ (p. 132)
1371.7   NY 17A, Bellvale, NY (p. 133)
Anton on the Lake $80D (p. 136)
845-477-0010
Maildrop: 7 Waterstone Rd., Greenwood Lake, NY 10925

Begin Map 22: 1372-1460 miles

DAY 89–5/27   12.4 OR 17.5 MILES
1371.7   NY 17A, Bellvale, NY (p. 133)
1384.1   AT on Arden Valley Rd. for 0.4 miles
1389.2   Arden Valley Rd., Tioati Circle (p. 138)
Back to Anton on the Lake

DAY 90–5/28   14.4 MILES

1389.2   Arden Valley Rd., Tioati Circle (p. 138)

1403.6   Bear Mtn. Bridge (p. 139)

Hudson River, Ft. Montgomery, NY

Bear Mtn. Bridge Motel (p. 140)

845-446-2472 $75 D   Call for pickup

Maildrop: POB 554, Ft. Montgomery, NY 10922

DAY 91–5/29   25.2 MILES

1403.6   Bear Mtn. Bridge (p. 139)

1428.8   Hortontown Rd., RPH Shelter (p. 142)

Call Martin & Donna Hunley for pickup: 845-505-1671
or 845-546-1832

To take us to Dutchess in Wingdale (p. 144)

Dutchess Motor Lodge—stay 2 nights

845-832-6400 or 914-525-9276 $73. Laundry $7. Free
ride when available.

Maildrop: 1512 Rt 22, Wingdale, NY 12594

DAY 92–5/30   19.6 MILES

1428.8   Hortontown Rd., RPH Shelter (p. 142)

1448.4   NY 22, Wingdale

Stay at Dutchess. Call them for pickup

Begin Map 23: 1460–1528 miles

DAY 93–5/31   18.7 MILES

1448.4   NY 22, Wingdale (p. 143)

1467.1   CT 341, Schaghticoke Rd., Kent, CT (p. 146)

Cooper Creek B&B (p. 148) $95 D Su-Thr

860-927-3508 Call for pickup. Also, see if they will take
us to laundry and dinner.

Day 94–6/1   15.9 MILES
1467.1   CT 341, Schaghticoke Rd., Kent, CT (p. 146)
1483.0   W. Cornwall Rd. (p. 147)
Bearded Woods (p. 150)
860-480-2966 Hudson and Big Lu

Day 95–6/2   16.2 MILES
1483.0   W. Cornwall Rd. (p. 147)
1499.2   Salisbury
Back at Bearded Woods

Day 96–6/3   ZERO

Day 97–6/4   13.4 OR 17.3 MILES
SOBO 16TH ANNIVERSARY
1499.2   Salisbury
1512.6   Guilder Pond, Mt. Everett Rd. (p. 152)
1516.5   Jug End Rd. (Looks like this is much closer
              with respect to the road. May be cheaper. Ask?)
Back at Bearded Woods

Day 98–6/5   12.9 MILES
1516.5   Jug End Rd.
1529.4   MA 23 (p. 153)
Jess Treat: 860-248-5710

Begin Map 24: 1528–1600 miles

Day 99–6/6   16.4 MILES
1529.4   MA 23 (p. 153)
1541.6   Main Rd. (p. 156)
1545.8   Goose Pond Rd. (gravel)

Back to Jess
Shuttle: David Ackerson: Bear Mtn. Bridge to Hanover
413-346-1033 or 413-652-9573

DAY 100–6/7   13.8 MILES
1545.8   Goose Pond Rd. (gravel)
1559.6   Washington Mtn. Rd. (p. 156)
Becket Motel (p. 158)
413-623-8888 will pick up at US 20 or Washington Mtn.
Rd.
Maildrop: 29 Chester Rd., Becket, MA 01223
We stayed at Jess Treat's place instead of moving to the
Becket Motel.

DAY 101–6/8   10.5 MILES
1559.6   Washington Mtn. Rd. (p. 156)
1570.1   AT on Gulf Rd./High St., Dalton, MA (p.
         157)
Shamrock Village Inn (p. 158), 413-684-0860

DAY 102–6/9   16.2 MILES
1570.1   AT on Gulf Rd./High St. (p. 157)
1586.3   Mt. Greylock (p. 160)
Bascom Lodge: 413-743-1591
Private room $125. No laundry.

DAY 103–6/10   6.3 MILES
1586.3   Mt. Greylock (p. 160)
1592.6   MA 2, Hoosic River (p. 160)
The Birches B&B $125D Free pickup/return (p. 163)
413-458-8134

Will slack to Bennington so stay 2 nights?
We stayed at the Williamstown Motel instead of The Birches B&B

Begin Map 25: 1592–1678 miles

Day 104–6/11   18.4 miles
SOBO?
1592.6   MA 2, Hoosic River (p. 160)
1611.0   VT 9 Bennington, VT (p. 161)
Stay back at Birches

Day 105–6/12   20.6 or 22.6 miles
1611.0   VT 9 Bennington, VT (p. 161)
1631.6   USFS 71
1633.6   Stratton–Arlington Rd., Manchester Center, VT (p. 166)
Green Mtn. House (p. 169) Free shuttle to trail. Maybe stay 2 nights. How far will they shuttle? Need to find out about next stop. Will Silas pick up?
330-338-6478 Jeff & Regina
Private Room
Or check out
The Lodge at Bromley $99 Ride to/from w/stay
802-824-6941
Maildrop: 4216 VT 11, Peru, VT 05152

Day 106–6/13   17.5 miles
1633.6   Stratton–Arlington Rd., Manchester Center, VT (p. 166)
1651.1   VT 11 & 30 (p. 167)
Stay at Green Mtn. House again

DAY 107–6/14   17.6 MILES

1651.1   VT 11 & 30 (p. 167)

1668.7   Danby–Landgrove Rd., Danby, VT (p. 170).
　　　　　Also called Brooklyn Rd. & USFS 10

*Silas Griffith B&B $99D. Will they pick up? If yes, stay 2
nights. (p. 169) 802-293-5567*

Maildrop: 178 S. Main St., Danby, VT 05739

Begin Map 26: 1678–1765 miles

DAY 108–6/15   14.8 OR 18.7 MILES
SOBO?

1668.7   Danby–Landgrove Rd., Danby, VT (p. 170).
　　　　　Also called Brooklyn Rd. & USFS 10

1683.5   VT 103 (p. 171)

1687.4   Cold River Rd. (p. 171)

Maybe stay at Silas again

*Maybe call Apex Shuttle (Stray Cat) to help: 603-252-
8294*

DAY 109–6/16   13.5 OR 15.4 MILES

1687.4   Cold River Rd. (p. 171)

1700.9   US 4, Rutland

1702.8   Sherburne Pass Trail (p. 174)

The Inn @ Long Trail (p. 172) 802-775-7181

Maildrop: 709 US 4, Killington, VT 05751

DAY 110–6/17   12.6 OR 21.4 MILES

1702.8   Sherburne Pass Trail (p. 174)

1715.4   Chateauguay Rd. (p. 174)

*Can Apex drop us off and we slack back to Inn @ Long
Trail? SOBO*

Or look for places to stay in Woodstock or just stay @ Long Trail Inn
1724.2 VT12, Barnard Gulf Rd. (p. 175) (not far from
       Woodstock)
Maybe call Apex Shuttle (Stray Cat) to help: 603-252-8294

DAY 111–6/18   21.4 MILES
1724.2 VT 12, Barnard Gulf Rd. (p. 175)
1745.6 Main St., Norwich (p. 180)
Norwich Inn
802-649-1143
Maildrop: 325 Main St., Norwich, VT 04055

DAY 112–6/19   ZERO AT NORWICH INN

DAY 113–6/20   19.0 MILES
1745.6 Main St., Norwich (p. 180)
1764.6 Grafton Turnpike (p. 181)
Dowd's Country Inn B&B $100D weekdays (p. 182)
603-795-4712 Pickup/return available
Ask about laundry?

Begin Map 27: 1765–1844 miles

DAY 114–6/21   16.1 MILES
SOBO?
1764.6 Grafton Turnpike (p. 181)
1780.7 NH 25A, Wentworth, NH (p. 181)
See if Dowd's will pickup if we stay 2 nights. If not may need to move ahead to Hiker's Welcome Hostel. See next.

Day 115–6/22　　9.8 miles

1780.7　NH 25A, Wentworth, NH (p. 181)
1790.5　NH 25, Oliverian Brook north of road (p 184)
Hiker's Welcome Hostel (p. 187) 603-989-0040
Maildrop: 1396 NH Rt 25, Glencliff, NH 03238

Day 116–6/23　　9.3 miles
SOBO Mt. Moosilauke

1790.5　NH 25, Oliverian Brook north of road (p. 184)
1799.8　Lost River Rd., NH 112, Kinsman Notch (p. 184)

Stay at Hiker's Welcome Hostel again or call Woodstock Inn or Gale River Motel
The Shuttle Connection: 603-745-3140 Also has laundry.
Woodstock Inn: 603-745-3951
Gale River Motel: 603-823-5655, 800-255-7989 Free pickup/return w/stay. Laundry $2. (Closer but opposite direction from Woodstock Inn.)

Day 117–6/24　　16.3 miles

1799.8　Lost River Rd., NH 112, Kinsman Notch (p. 184)
1815.9　US 3, I-93, AT underpass. Town east on US 3, better to take side trail (next entry)
1816.1　Franconia Notch
Woodstock Inn: 603-745-3951
Gale River Motel: 603-823-5655

Day 118–6/25　　ZERO

Woodstock Inn: 603-745-3951 or Gale River Motel: 603-823-5655

DAY 119–6/26   13 MILES
1816.1 Franconia Notch (p. 185)
1829.1 Frost Trail to Galehead Hut (p. 190) AMC:
603-466-2727 (www.outdoors.org)

DAY 120–6/27   14.7 MILES
1829.1 Galehead Hut
1843.8 Crawford Notch, US 302 (p. 190)
Woodstock Inn: 603-745-3951 or Gale River Motel: 603-823-5655

Begin Map 28: 1844–1922 miles

DAY 121–6/28   12.5 MILES
1843.8 Crawford Notch, US 302 (p. 190)
1856.3 Mt. Washington
White Mtn. Lodge. (p. 197) Can Marney pick us up or should we hitch a ride down?
603-466-5049. Has private room.

DAY 122–6/29   13.5 MILES
SOBO WOULD BE GREAT
1856.3 Mt. Washington
1869.8 NH 16, Pinkham Notch
White Mtn. Lodge. (p. 197) again

DAY 123–6/30   5.9 OR 21.1 MILES
1869.8 NH 16, Pinkham Notch (p. 194)
1875.7 Nineteen Mile Brook Trail–Carter Moriah
         Trail, Carter Notch Hut 0.1E
1890.9 US 2, Gorham (p. 195)
White Mtn. again

DAY 124–7/1   ZERO @ WHITE MTN.

DAY 125–7/2   11.8 OR 17 MILES
1890.9   US 2, Gorham (p. 195)
1902.7   Gentian Pond Shelter (p. 195)
1907.9   Carlo Col Shelter (p. 198)
TENT
We did not have to tent. We worked with Earl at The Cabin to slack us from US 2, Gorham to Rangeley.

Begin Map 29: 1907–1955 miles

DAY 126–7/3   15.1 MILES
1907.9   Carlo Col Shelter (p. 198)
1922.0   Grafton Notch, ME 26 (p. 198)
Pine Ellis Lodging Private Rooms $60D (p. 202) Ilene & David
207-392-4161. Shuttles from Grafton Notch to Rangeley.
Maildrop: 20 Pine St., Andover, ME 04216
We stayed at The Cabin instead of Pine Ellis

DAY 127–7/4   10.3 MILES
1922.0   Grafton Notch, ME 26 (p. 198)
1932.3   East B Hill Rd. (p. 199)
Pine Ellis Lodging again

DAY 128–7/5   10.1 MILES
1932.3   East B Hill Rd. (p. 199)
1942.4   South Arm Rd.
Pine Ellis Lodging again

DAY 129–7/6   13.2 MILES
1942.4   South Arm Rd.
1955.6   ME 17, Oquossoc (p. 200)
Farmhouse Inn
Shane—Private Room, 207-864-3113
Maildrop: 2057 Main St., Rangeley, ME 04970

Begin Map 30: 1955-2001 miles

DAY 130–7/7   13.2 MILES
1955.6   ME 17, Oquossoc (p. 200)
1968.8   ME 4, Rangeley (p. 201)
Back to Farmhouse

DAY 131–7/8   13.5 MILES
SOBO
1968.8   ME 4, Rangeley (p. 201)
1982.3   Woods Rd. (p. 201)
Back to Farmhouse

DAY 132–7/9   18.7 MILES
1982.3   Woods Rd.
2001.0   ME 27 Stratton, ME (p. 204)
Stratton Motel $60 Private Room (p. 208)
207-246-4171
Slacking available
Maildrop:
See if it makes sense to slack back here vs move onto Mtn.
Village Farm B&B ahead
162 Main St., Stratton, ME 04982

Begin Map 31: 2001–2038 miles

DAY 133–7/10   16.7 OR 19.5 MILES

2001.0   ME 27 Stratton, ME (p. 204)

2017.7   E. Flagstaff Rd. (p. 205)

2020.5   Long Falls Dam Rd.

Mtn. Village Farm B&B 207-265-2030 (p. 208) Will pick up $40

We stayed an extra day at the Stratton Motel instead of moving to Mtn. Village Farm B&B

DAY 134–7/11   17.5 MILES

2020.5   E. Flagstaff Rd. (p. 205)

2038.0   US 201, Caratunk, ME (p. 206) Ferry 9–11 & 2–4 July 10–Sep 30.

Northern Outdoors—Free shuttle coordinated with ferry 800-765-7238

Maildrop: 1771 US 201, The Forks, ME 04985

We stayed at The Sterling Inn instead of Northern Outdoors.

Fletcher Mtn. Outfitters: David Corrigan provides shuttles: 207-672-4879

Begin Map 32: 2038–2074 miles

DAY 135–7/12   11.9 MILES

2038.0   US 201, Caratunk, ME (p. 206)

2049.9   Moxie Pond South (p. 207) Also called Troutdale Rd. Pickup near Joes Hole

Back to Northern Outdoors

Call David for shuttle 207-672-4879

DAY 136–7/13   10.8 MILES
2049.9   Moxie Pond South
2060.7   Bald Mtn. Rd. (p. 207) If not reachable then
             onto Shirley–Blanchard Rd. for 18.5-mile day
Shaw's Lodging $35 private room (p. 212)
207-997-3597. Call for pickup.
Maildrop: 17 Pleasant St., Monson, ME 04464

DAY 137–7/14   14 MILES
2060.7   Bald Mtn. Rd. (p. 207)
2074.7   ME 15, Monson (p. 210)
Back to Shaw's

Begin Map 33: 2074–2105 miles

100-MILE WILDERNESS
Shaw's will work the front end (207-997-3597) and Paul
(OldMan) and Jaime (NaviGator) Renaud 207-723-
4321 for slacking through the wilderness
OldMan and NaviGator has The Appalachian Trail Lodge
207-723-4321 $55 Private Room
Maildrop: 33 Penobscot Ave., Millinocket, ME 04462

DAY 138–7/15   15.3 + 0.8 MILES
2074.7   ME 15, Monson (p. 210)
2090.0   Trail 0.8 to Otter Pond parking
Shaw to pickup/dropoff

DAY 139–7/16   0.8 + 14.5 MILES
2090.0   Trail 0.8 to Otter Pond parking
2104.5   Katahdin Ironworks Rd. (gravel) (p. 211)
Either Shaw or OldMan/NaviGator pickup/dropoff

Begin Map 34: 2105–2140 miles

DAY 140–7/17   14.9 MILES
2104.5   Katahdin Ironworks Rd. (gravel) (p. 211)
2119.4   Logan Brook Rd. (dirt)
OldMan/NaviGator pickup/dropoff all the way to Katahdin

DAY 141–7/18   13.7 MILES
2119.4   Logan Brook Rd. (dirt)
2133.1   Jo-Mary Rd. (p. 215)

Begin Map 35: 2140–2190 miles

DAY 142–7/19   22.5 MILES
2133.1   Jo-Mary Rd. (p. 215)
2156.6   Pollywog Stream

DAY 143–7/20   17.5 MILES
2156.6   Pollywog Stream
2174.1   Abol Bridge (p. 219)

DAY 144–7/21   9.9 MILES
2174.1   Abol Bridge
2184.0   KSC

DAY 145–7/22   5.2 MILES + RETURN
2184.0   KSC
2189.2   Katahdin

Appendix II
Draft Mail Drop List

(with Maps to include)

Map 1–3: Take to RE & Gay's
Springer through Smokies (0–238 miles)
Day 1–19; February 28 to March 18

Map 4: Alan to bring to Newfound Gap
End of Smokies to Erwin (238–352 miles)
Day 20–26; March 19 to 25

Map 5: Cantarroso Farm, 777 Bailey Lane, Erwin, TN 37650
423-833-7514
Erwin to Damascus (352–469 miles)
Day 27–34; March 16 to April 2
Mail Date: March 10

Map 6–7: Lazy Fox B&B, 133 Imboden Street, Damascus, VA 24236

276-475-5838

Damascus to Pearisburg (469–636 miles)

Day 35–44; April 3 to 12

Mail Date: March 27

Map 8–9: Woods Hole Hostel, 3696 Sugar Run Rd., Pearisburg, VA 24134

540-921-3444

Pearisburg to Rockfish Gap (632–861 miles)

Day 45–58; April 13 to 26

Will come home for April 21 doctor's appt.

Mail Date: April 6

Map 10–12: Tree Streets Inn, 421 Walnut Ave., Waynesboro, VA 22980

540-949-4484

Rockfish Gap to Front Royal (861–970 miles)

Day 59–64; April 27 to May 2

Mail Date: April 20

Map 13–14: Front Royal Terrapin Station Hostel, 304 Chester Gap Rd, Chester Gap, VA 22623

540-539-0509

Front Royal to Harpers Ferry (970–1027 miles)

Day 65–67; May 3 to 5

Mail Date: April 27

Map 15–16: ATC HQ, 799 Washington St, Harpers Ferry, WV 25425
Harpers Ferry to Pen Mar (MD–PA line) (1024–1082 miles)
Day 68–70; May 6 to 8
Mail Date: April 27

Map 17–18: Scottish Inn & Suites, 5651 Lincoln Way East, Fayetteville, PA 17222
717-352-2144, 800-251-1962
Pen Mar to Duncannon (1082–1174 miles)
Day 71–75: May 9 to 13
Mail Date: May 1

Map 19–20: Allenberry Resort Inn, 1559 Boiling Spring Rd., Boiling Springs, PA 17007
800-430-5468
Duncannon to Delaware Water Gap (1147–1294 miles)
Day 76–83; May 14 to 21
Mail Date: May 6

Map 21: Edge of the Woods Outfitters, 110 Main St, Delaware Water Gap, PA 18327
Delaware Water Gap to Antons on the Lake (1294–1372 miles)
Day 84–88; May 21 to 26
Mail Date: May 12

Map 22: Anton on the Lake, 7 Waterstone Rd, Greenwood Lake, NY 10925

845-477-0010

Anton of the Lake to NY–CT line (1372–1460 miles)

Day 89–92; May 27 to 30

Mail Date: May 19

Map 23: Dutchess Motor Lodge, 1512 Rt 22, Wingdale, NY 12594

845-832-6400 or 914-525-9276

NY-CT Line to MA–VT Line (1460–1528 miles)

Day 93–98; May 31 to June 5

Mail Date: May 22

Map 24–26: Jess Treat, 95 Maple Ave., Sheffield, MA 01257

860-248-5710

MA/VT Line to Grafton Turnpike, NH (1528–1765 miles)

Day 99–113; June 5 to 20

Mail Date: May 27

Map 27–28: Norwich Inn, 325 Main St., Norwich, VT 04055

802-649-1143

Grafton Turnpike, NH to Grafton Notch (1765–1922 miles)

Day 105–126; June 21 to July 3

Mail Date: June 15

Map 29–32: Pine Ellis Lodging, 20 Pine Street, Andover, ME 04216

207-392-4161
Grafton Notch to Monson (1907–2074 miles)
Day 127–137; July 4 to 14
Mail Date: June 26

Map 33–35: Shaw's Lodging, 17 Pleasant St., Monson, ME 04464

207-997-3597
Monson to Katahdin (2047–2190 miles)
Day 138–145; July 15 to 22
Mail Date: July 6

Meet the Authors

Lelia Vann and Greg Reck live in Norfolk, Virginia. Lelia had dreams of thru-hiking the Appalachian Trail but never felt she could take six months of leave from her job with NASA. After her brother, who was a retired National Forest Service ranger, said he would thru-hike the trail with her, she decided to retire at 55 so she could fulfill her dream.

Originally, Greg, also a NASA retiree, was going to support them but soon decided it would be more fun to hike with them. After their first thru-hike of the Appalachian Trail in 2014, they decided to thru-hike again in 2015, but this time they wanted to slack pack as much as they could and document the cost of lodging and transportation.

In 2016, they attempted their third thru-hike but had to be rescued in the White Mountains of New Hampshire. They are currently planning their fourth thru-hike in 2017.

9 780997 522631